# How to be a
# Successful Teacher

# How to be a Successful Teacher

## Strategies for Personal and Professional Development

Paul Castle and Scott Buckler

Los Angeles | London | New Delhi
Singapore | Washington DC

SAGE Publications Ltd
1 Oliver's Yard
55 City Road
London EC1Y 1SP

SAGE Publications Inc.
2455 Teller Road
Thousand Oaks, California 91320

SAGE Publications India Pvt Ltd
B 1/I 1 Mohan Cooperative Industrial Area
Mathura Road
New Delhi 110 044

SAGE Publications Asia-Pacific Pte Ltd
33 Pekin Street #02-01
Far East Square
Singapore 048763

**Library of Congress Control Number: 2009924024**

**British Library Cataloguing in Publication data**

A catalogue record for this book is available from the British Library

ISBN 0 978-1-84920-016-5
ISBN 0 978-1-84920-017-2 (pbk)

Typeset by C&M Digitals (P) Ltd, Chennai, India
Printed in India at Replika Press Pvt Ltd
Printed on paper from sustainable resources

# Contents

# About the authors

**Dr Paul Castle** is a Chartered Sport and Exercise Psychologist at the University of Worcester. He obtained his doctorate from the University of Warwick and his doctoral thesis explored psychophysiology and cross-modality perception. Paul's consultancy work involves specializing in using applied psychology to help clients improve their performance in a wide range of domains within and beyond sport. Paul is author of *Psychology of Motorsport Success* and has research publications ranging from olfaction (smell), to stress (neutrophil activation), through to learning and teaching (student-centred feedback). Paul also has a competitive interest in cycle time trialling (where 'coping strategies' are everything).

**Scott Buckler** originally trained as a primary school teacher, teaching in London and Birmingham before pursuing a career in higher education. His research interests have previously encompassed special education needs, applied education and educational experiences beyond the curriculum. He has developed this last theme through his doctoral work in transpersonal psychology (specifically into self-transcendence), and also through his professional interest of facilitating student growth whatever their age. Scott is co-author of *Your Dissertation in Education* (published by Sage) and has research publications ranging from learning and teaching, occupational stress, to the martial arts. Scott has a keen interest in this last area, especially the psychotherapeutic elements (where keeping 'mindful' and 'focused' are essential while training and while teaching).

# Acknowledgements

The authors would like to thank the many people who have provided their support in bringing this book together. Indeed this book would not have been written without the discussions with teachers, colleagues and students, past and present. Such people have helped inspire this book and indirectly will benefit students to come.

Paul would like to thank Gaye Arnold for her input at the conceptual stage of this project. Without your enthusiastic fervour for the need to unleash this concept on 'the world', the project may have been consigned to the proverbial waste basket. Serendipity is indeed a great thing! To Mick Donovan, Institute of Sport and Exercise Science, University of Worcester, whose support at a critical moment in the writing process was much appreciated. Also, to Nicola, whose experiences having undertaken the PGCE primary course at Worcester University during 2008/09, served to confirm the need for this book in supporting PQT's and NQT's through such a challenging period. Enjoy the book! Use it wisely in your NQT year and beyond ... and control the controllables!

Scott would like to thank Roger Lawrence and Jean Lane, who are actively held responsible for his taste for teaching; his love for learning. Their impact resounds to this day ... and beyond. Furthermore, Genea Rawcliffe, a wonderful friend and outstanding teacher and lecturer, for her advice and counsel from the outset. To the staff and students within the Institute of Education at University of Worcester particularly Professor Chris Robertson and Dr Hugh Somervell, who have offered support in so many different ways. Also to Claire, who has never questioned the need to disappear into my writing hole for extended periods, while also providing unending encouragement (and cups of coffee!) at crucial times.

We would both like to thank Nick Boot-Handford for preparing previous versions of several schematic diagrams that appear in the book and Claire Buckler for producing the new schematic diagrams. Furthermore, Phil Beadle for his foreword: an inspiration to all teachers (and a University of Worcester alumni).

Finally, we would like to acknowledge the support and guidance from everyone at Sage Publications, especially Dr Helen Fairlie whose committed belief and continual support has enabled our ideas to become a reality. May we wish you well for the future.

# Preface

Teaching is one of the most exciting professions in which to be to be involved. Whether working with younger children, older children, students or adult education, facilitating a learner's process is extremely rewarding. Alongside the many positives of the profession, teaching is challenging resulting in continued questioning. Indeed, we could stress that a professional is someone who continually asks: What am I doing? How am I doing it? Why am I doing it? With the ever-changing nature of education, how can you develop and thrive within your chosen profession over the coming years, ensuring that you enjoy each moment in the classroom?

Despite many books being written for teachers where theories and principles of psychology are applied for learners, few, if any, actually focus on the applied psychological skills required by the teacher. Furthermore, due to the time constraints on the delivery of teacher training, such topics are seldom covered on courses. This book is a handbook to guide teachers in their formative years of teaching experience. By 'formative years', this could be from your first day of teacher training, through to the first few years of paid employment.

The text has been designed to be readily accessible to a wider audience, across all age phases both nationally and internationally. As a result, no prior knowledge of psychology is needed, although we appreciate that your teacher training would have probably covered a number of applied psychological aspects for use with students.

The text is organized into distinct yet complementary sections and is written in such a way so that you can select any chapter and make progress, depending on your needs at the time. We equate this to a 'bricks and mortar' analogy: in order to build a wall it is important to set appropriate foundations (Chapter 1); have a supply of bricks (individual chapters and the strategies within) and an amount of mortar (cross-referencing between chapters). In building the wall, it does not matter which brick is selected at any given point (as they are all equitable). Rather, it is the mortar, holding these bricks together that is important for the stability of the wall.

Section 1 provides an overview of important psychological themes (for example, confidence), that may impact on teaching performance. Section 2 explores physical issues related to successful psychological functioning, such as fitness and nutrition, both of which are vital to successful psychological performance. Section 3 shows the reader how to learn and use psychological skills techniques directly. Section 4 integrates the material presented in the previous sections and provides concluding remarks on using psychological skills and techniques in a progressive way to improve teaching performance.

This book actually came about through using psychology to our advantage to turn disillusion into something more positive. One morning in early April, we met up for a coffee and were demoralized. The term was over so we were missing student contact. Individual projects we had been working on had come to fruition yet instead of being ecstatic, we were at a loss. Over a cappuccino we decided to put our respective experience to good use into the book you are now holding. Paul is an experienced chartered psychologist who has worked extensively in the field of education and sport. Scott has worked across different age phases as a teacher and has an academic interest in applied psychology within the classroom, specifically to engage and empower students.

Ultimately we are both are interested in ensuring that you are able to gain the same rewards from the teaching profession as us, to achieve the highest possible standards, to enjoy and thrive in the classroom. It is this aim which has driven this book.

Paul Castle and Scott Buckler
April 2009

# Foreword

## Daniel Goleman's Either/Or

Daniel Goleman, in his book *Emotional Intelligence*, asks the reader to imagine they are on a plane, and the pilot comes on the intercom. 'We are coming up to some turbulence,' he calmly says, 'Fasten your seat belts ladies and gentlemen. It's going to get very rough indeed.' And when the turbulence comes it's far worse than anyone would have thought. The plane feels as if it's falling out of the sky. It makes huge, gut-wrenching swoops and drops. Rain thrashes the wings, as it lurches upward and, from thence down, down, down; a sickening rollercoaster with neither wheels nor safety net.

Put yourself in this situation. You are a passenger on this plane. Do you …

## Either …
Look at the other passengers to see how scared they are. Keep the window blind up to see how near the lightning is getting to the plane. Scan the safety instructions in detail, poring your eyes over every word before they dart nervously in the direction of the cabin crew. Looking at them for any signs that the hostesses are genuinely worried that they too are going to die.

## Or …
Read a magazine. Have a look at the in-flight film … anything to take your mind off the fact you might be going to die in the next few minutes.

Who has the better time here? Either, *either* or, erm, *or*. It's what they call on television a no-brainer. Repetitive cycles of worry just make us feel worse. The person who has a practised ability to distract themselves in moments of stress, who is able to accentuate the positive, so Goleman tells us, is more likely to be able to control their hormonal surges, more likely to be able to function to a high level, and will have much more fun. And after all, work has got to be fun hasn't it? Otherwise y'know, it's just that: work!

## This book

The book you have in your hands is the difference between either and or. It is the difference between repetitive cycles of worry and positivity linked to action. For you, the reader, it could be the difference between losing your sense of humour with a kid, and getting the kid to lose it with laughter.

Paul and Scott's book gives teachers, whether they be fresh, bright faces new to the game, or hardened old hacks likes this writer, the opportunity to learn from the world of academic psychology. Great teachers are instinctively psychologically attuned to their students' needs, but we are rarely analytical about what we do in this field. Doing the exercises over the following chapters will give you, dear educator, an opportunity to apply the terms and techniques from another discipline to our own. Reading it may change your attitude to your students, your colleagues and, most of all, to yourself. It is written accessibly and has a pleasingly irreverent tone, but a warning: it will challenge you to think differently!

Read it from the middle outwards, from the front to the back; or read it by randomly selecting one page a day. But make sure you read it with a pen or a highlighter in hand. With this book you learn by doing.

Phil Beadle

# How to use this book

## Contentious statement 1: Books are boring!

We've read enough of them in our time so we're talking from our own limited perspective. Sure, we have read 'classic' books, books we have been required to read for courses, books we have read for our own preparation … We have even been known to read books for enjoyment! However on reflection we have realized that the best books are the ones that actively engage us, those which demand a dialogue, whether guessing 'whodunit' or those which cause us to pause and reflect.

This 'activeness' is something that appeals to us: whether this is due to our subject disciplines, or whether this is due to a limited concentration span! With this in mind, we have approached this book in a way we would like to read it.

This book is designed to be read in different ways. Some may opt for the 'traditional' approach of starting at the first page and progressing through to the last. Alternatively, you may opt for 'dipping in' – reading the chapters that are personally relevant at the moment as discussed previously with the bricks and mortar analogy. The introductory chapter does, however, set the scene for the book and would be worth reading before any other.

To get the most out of this book we ask you to engage with the activities and reflections, to take time to pause and assess how the information relates to you personally. One way to ensure this is to ask you to purchase a new notebook and pen which you keep alongside this book, so that you can engage with the activities as they arise. You may prefer to keep a binder of some sort where you can create a portfolio of activities, while supplementing the material with other things you find. Perhaps in this technologically advanced age, you would prefer to use your phone/laptop/pda hybrid! Whatever you choose, engage with the activities as they arise. (Alas we will not ask you to submit your journal for assessment or scrutiny – you can breathe a sigh of relief!)

Throughout the book, each chapter develops in the same format:

- *Introduction:* to inform you of the nature and content of the chapter.
- *Chapter objectives:* to detail what you should have developed through engaging with the chapter.
- *One-minute summary:* to provide a reflective overview of the chapter.

- *Short-term strategies for the here and now:* this section title shows exactly what these strategies are designed to do – provide instant results. However, the chapter (and, holistically, the book) will help ensure long-term solutions.
- *Mentoring issues:* aspects you may want to discuss with your mentor.
- *Further reading:* to highlight additional resources to deepen and develop your understanding and interest. Please note that these resources are a 'flavour' of what is available and not an exhaustive list. As such, these resources are subject to our own preferences, and so on.

In addition, the majority of the chapters contain the following:

- *Reflection:* these ask you to consider how various elements we discuss relate to your experience.
- *Activities:* the tasks are to enable you to engage with some of the theoretical aspects discussed in the chapter, a chance to 'try things out for yourself'.
- *Summary boxes:* which review key aspects from the chapter.
- *Key statements:* throughout the book in bold italics which highlight important concepts.
- *Case studies:* occasionally a case study is cited to demonstrate the practical nature of the chapter.

## Website
In addition to the words within this book, there are a number of other resources that may be found on the supporting website, for example:

- Resource sheets: these files will help facilitate some of the activities we discuss in this book and will aid your development.
- MP3 files: the files consist of additional material to supplement the chapters, for example, downloadable relaxation scripts for a variety of concepts we have raised.
- Video files: the videos help to demonstrate certain concepts we have discussed in the book.

The website may be found at: www.sucessfulteacher.org

## Terminology

This book has been written so that as many teachers as possible may access it, nationally and internationally. To this extent, examples have been kept generic to enable you to relate these to your practice; however, at times where we feel a specific example is warranted, we may provide a context you are unfamiliar with. Furthermore, we have opted for the term 'student' as opposed to child or pupil, to represent any learner you may have responsibility for.

## Academic-ness of this book

Please keep in mind that this book is written to enable you to develop the relevant strategies for success in the classroom. To this extent, we have opted for a more informal style than you may be used to with 'academic' books. There are many theoretical perspectives we could have introduced and/or elaborated on; however, we have intentionally provided 'just enough' theory to contextualize the practical aspects. It is these practical aspects that we have honed through our experience of working with teachers and students which we feel are fundamental to this book.

## Pass the book on!

Finally, we would like to encourage you to pass the book on. We see books as gifts, pages that bring wisdom and advice when you need it. On several occasions, people have given us books 'just at the right time' – whether to help with research, whether they have enjoyed the read and want us to get that same enjoyment. Don't just keep the knowledge contained within these pages to yourself – help others to get the most from their teaching as we hope you get from yours.

May we wish you every success for this new venture ... You may now turn to the first chapter (unless you are going for the postmodern approach to reading).

# Section 1

# Psychological aspects

The first section of the book introduces a range of the most commonly occurring psychological aspects relating to performance in the classroom. Chapter 1 introduces applied psychology and encourages you to think of the issues you may have previously covered in your training and development, while also introducing you to the structure of the book. It develops by encouraging you to think of the strengths and challenges within your professional practice while also asking you to consider what the 'ideal' teacher is.

Chapter 2 explores concentration and attention. Keeping your mind focused on the task at hand is crucial within teaching, not only to maximize your time but also to minimize disruption from other sources. This chapter makes reference to other chapters within the book to equip you to ensure that the time you spend on your planning, preparation and assessment is of high quality yet limited in quantity.

Chapter 3 discusses motivation, a key aspect responsible for a teacher's performance in the classroom. Although motivation is a complex subject, we have identified some key areas demonstrating how motivation can be influenced negatively while providing strategies to develop motivation levels should they start to suffer.

Chapter 4 highlights the importance of confidence and self-esteem, two fundamental areas that teachers need to exhibit on a daily basis. Again we look at factors that may affect confidence and self-esteem, how to recognize if this is happening and how to resolve any issues through the strategies included.

Chapter 5 examines the way in which emotion, mood and stress influence performance, furthermore examining how they relate. Stress is a worrying trend that is increasing within education according to recent research, so being able to recognize where stress can come from, how stress can have an impact, and ways in which stress can be negated are discussed within this chapter.

The final chapter of this section, Chapter 6, deals with the one thing we can be sure of within education ... continual change. It is flippantly noted that 'there are no new ideas in education' or that 'education evolves on a 20-year cycle'. What was 'fashionable' a decade or so back may have become equally fashionable now. Furthermore, given that the

National Curriculum appears to be changed every three years or so, and it appears a new government initiative needs introducing on a weekly basis, and so on, being able to adapt to change is a key component of a teacher's ability.

# 1

# The Morning Bell: Another Day Begins! Introduction

## Introduction to psychology

Psychology impacts on every minute of every day of our lives. The decisions we make are founded upon our thoughts, beliefs, principles and morals. Our decisions are influenced by a range of emotional states. If we feel frustrated, we are more likely to be frustrated with every minor annoyance which in turn is likely to be detrimental to our performance. Loss of concentration, fatigue or a lack of self-confidence can occur at the most inopportune times, resulting in a similar poor performance. There are days when we may lack passion, drive and motivation. Thankfully, for each of these states, there seems to be an opposite – where we have an unshakeable confidence, where we operate in a clear, focused and energized state. Yet day after day we are expected to perform to the best of our abilities where it counts ... in the classroom. Psychology thus informs (or misinforms) what we think and how we act or react in the various situations that arise in the classroom (and of course outside).

The key is to ensure we can maximize our psychological resources, to ensure that we are operating at our optimum level to enable ourselves, and in turn our students, to get the most from the wondrous experience of teaching and learning. Yet how can this be achieved?

In order to thrive within the classroom, the secret is to ensure consistency: to embrace all of your psychological resources (both positive and negative) which in turn will allow you to acknowledge the elements that you need to succeed as a teacher. Furthermore, it is necessary to develop the required skills to become psychologically strong when it matters. This is what the chapters in this book will help to facilitate.

## Chapter objectives

- Consider how psychology is included in education.
- Reflect on how you reward and punish yourself professionally.
- Understand the basics of Psychological Skills Training.
- Identify professional 'challenges'.
- Develop a picture of the 'ideal' teacher.

## Psychology of education

For a number of years, there have been developing areas of research within the psychology of education. To the greater extent this research has focused on using psychology to 'enable' learners, for example through principles of effective teaching and learning, behaviour management, supporting individual needs, and so on. Yet in relation, little research exists specifically for the teacher in developing their personal 'toolbox'. To some extent, this is expected to be 'picked up' during your lengthy apprenticeship to the classroom with little guidance provided by tutors, mentors or colleagues as to how to strive and survive the profession.

We do appreciate that in your training there are so many elements to cover that you may not have had much input into developing your personal skills and strategies. However, you have got this far in your chosen career, so we would like to think you have a number of skills and strategies in place – indeed this book is written on the assumption that you have!

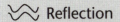 Reflection

- Consider your time either training to be a teacher or your professional development since becoming a teacher.
- Draw a set of scales (or a see-saw). What 'weighting' would you give to the amount of psychology discussed in your course for:
  o theories and principles of teaching and learning;
  o personal skills and strategies development.
- Provide examples under each as to what you covered.

## The carrot and the stick – do you have vision or do you 'beat yourself up'?

Teaching is a rewarding career. We make this statement from our personal experience and the experience we have heard time and time again from colleagues and students. Whatever age range you are working with, you will experience the joy of enabling others. Yet counter to this, teaching can cause worries, worries we can punish ourselves with continuously, whether it is a session that didn't quite fit together, to inspectors coming in, or not having enough hours in the day! It is hard to think of any other career where the rewards and punishments are meted out by our very selves, day in, day out. Yet this is what makes teaching the ultimate profession, one where we continue to challenge ourselves, to become the best we can, to continually question what we are doing, how we are doing it and why we are doing it.

This continual change certainly prevents stagnation; however, it can also be a cause of duress where we are continually thinking what could go wrong, what has gone wrong, what has worked well, what could work better. *It is the focusing on WHAT you are doing that is important – this is what is within your control and is far more likely to lead to a successful result*. This is such an important message to keep in mind from this chapter onwards, a message we will return to through out this book.

> Keep focused on the here and now. This is what is known as 'mindfulness' – the 'mind' being 'full' of the present moment. This will be discussed further in Chapter 2.

Keeping your mind focused on the present, what you are actually doing, helps limit the worry about tomorrow or the next lesson, or an incident that happened last week. Focusing on things other than the present can drain your resources and prevent you from engaging with the task at hand. For example, you could sit there worrying about the pile of marking you have to complete, or you could just make a start on it.

 Activity 1.1

- Make a list of the 'rewards' you get from teaching. (Consider different domains: personal, professional, psychological, and so on.)
- Make a list of how you 'punish' yourself if things go wrong. (This could be continually worrying about things that may go wrong, even if they do not!)
- Allocate a weighting to the rewards and punishments (for example, 80:20 or 70:30, and so on).
- Consider the implications of the weighting: can you affect the balance? How?

## How can psychology help *you* succeed in the classroom?

The key perspective we have adopted throughout this book is a cognitive-behavioural approach. This means that, through the theme of this book, we aim to guide you in examining and changing **the way in which you think** about your teaching (the cognitive component). Sometimes, however, a 'quick fix' is required, where we will examine the way in which you might **react** in certain situations (the behavioural component). Behaviour that is cause for concern may then be modified or adapted appropriately to improve your performance in these situations.

The focus on the way you may react, the behavioural component, is an approach we call the 'elastoplast technique' because it does little more than solve the problem temporarily. It is not a definitive solution. By analogy, you may take a painkiller when you have a headache because it is a 'quick fix', but it is always best to establish what caused it in the first place so that it can be prevented in the future. Similarly within the classroom, you may intervene when two students are arguing (the quick fix) but may then invite the students to discuss their perception of the reasons for their altercation when things are more settled.

## Acknowledging 'weaknesses'

Humans generally don't like to admit that they have a weakness, let alone admit that they have a psychological weakness. Negative connotations are often associated with such psychological weakness, yet the stigma is unhelpful. Perhaps it would be better to rephrase 'weakness' into 'challenge' as it provides more positive connotations, that with work we can overcome the challenge. Indeed as teachers, we acknowledge the areas for improvement while celebrating the areas for success: we don't get too caught up on what a student is unable to do – we look at what they can do. The same is true for any of the themes within this book. If you lack knowledge or attributes about any aspect we discuss, it might simply mean that you have never thought it important, or even that you were never aware that it would help your teaching. Simply acknowledging the importance of psychology in your teaching is not enough. It is crucial that the psychological skills techniques that you will acquire through this book are practised until they become second nature, that you acknowledge your present 'psychological starting point'.

One way in which to develop is through Psychological Skills Training (PST) which will help you develop your present psychological foundations. Psychological Skills Training is a systematic, educational programme designed to help you acquire and practise performance-enhancing psychological skills. It offers a positive approach, focusing on the acquisition of new skills to address the 'challenge' rather than focusing on what teachers should not be doing. *As soon as you recognize that psychological skills can be used to improve your performance within the classroom, you have taken your first reflective step towards progress*. As you progress through this book, you will learn how to develop these skills, practise them, and incorporate them into your 'teaching brain'. By using PST successfully, the aim is to be able to be at the peak of optimal performance as the bell sounds for the first lesson.

〰 **Reflection**

- Consider your current performance in the classroom in relation to your psychological skills. Take a typical working week and the various tasks you conduct.
  - Note down any aspects you excel at (for example, perhaps you always meet deadlines).
  - Note down any aspects you find challenging (for example, being motivated to complete marking).
- By noting down these aspects, you have started to identify potential areas for improvement.

## Openness and honesty

In reading this book, it is imperative that you are open and honest with yourself in your thoughts about your ability and performance in the classroom. By this, we mean that you should try to consider the 'full picture' of your situation. Indeed, this may take time to develop and is not something to be completed in a few minutes. Often we can ignore the more pressing issues as we do not necessarily want to face them, or we may be completely unaware of them. Indeed, professionals who use psychology are trained to explore various 'avenues' in order to gain sufficient information to help resolve any emerging issues. Obviously this is not possible within a book. However, in order to gain maximum benefit, you should feel comfortable enough to think about the type of information you might need to be open and honest with in order to make progress. This book will help you to consider some of the possible difficulties you may be experiencing.

You will get the most from this book if you evaluate yourself at a personal level. This is the level at which you would not share your thoughts with anyone else at all. This is the level of complete honesty. If your performance as a teacher is suffering, this book should provide possible solutions as you become more honest with yourself. There may, however, be occasions when you do not wish to acknowledge that you may be at fault: few people like to accept this! Yet the successful teacher will be the one who accepts and evaluates their 'challenges', develops ways around these and moves on having learnt from them. *Consequently, such 'faults' or 'challenges' are nothing more than a label for something that needs to be changed in order to make improvement*. If teachers can accept this, there is no longer any need for negative feelings which, in turn, can cause further psychological 'challenges'.

## Ethical principles

Complementing openness and honesty, we should also mention the ethical principles contained within this book. In writing a book of this nature, our sole purpose is to enable self-empowerment through engaging with the various chapters, in turn facilitating your continued and future successes in the classroom. The methods and techniques within this book have been carefully considered in line with our professional and academic perspective, and as such, we acknowledge our responsibility for including these.

If you feel that there are areas you would like to explore further, in addition to the suggested readings, it may be necessary to seek professional support. Consultation with your general practitioner or a professional psychologist may be avenues to explore and we would make the point that this book may be used as a guide to overcoming challenges of a 'non-clinical' nature.

Although we discuss various 'cases' we have worked with in this book, at all times we have respected confidentiality in accordance with the ethical principles we operate under.

## The 'ideal' teacher

We would like to raise a question as to why you are reading this book. You probably picked it up because you are interested in becoming the best teacher you can become ... but do you know what that looks like? Perhaps you have in mind a teacher from your own time as a pupil who you would like to model yourself on. Perhaps you have been inspired by a teacher you have met on your training? Perhaps it is a teacher from the media or literature, for example Robin Williams's portrayal of John Keating in *Dead Poets Society*. Perhaps it is an eclectic mix of a number of teachers where you would take their best elements. Perhaps it is an ideal picture of you and who you could become. Which is better?

 **Activity 1.2**

- Draw a human outline. Illustrate it any way you would like. This is a picture of your 'ideal' teacher.
- Note down the attributes that make this 'ideal' teacher.
- Consider yourself as this 'ideal' teacher at some point in the future. Try to visualize how you are working within the classroom, or outside.
- Keep coming back to this picture from time to time, adding supplementary attributes, while acknowledging the attributes you have developed.
- We will return to mental imagery in Chapter 11.

## One-minute summary

In this introductory chapter, we have set the scene by providing an idea of how the way in which you think can affect your performance. We have also shown how the role of psychology can be embraced in your day-to-day teaching. By applying subtle changes and through engaging in the various exercises, you are already applying psychology and in turn focusing on successful teaching.

Metaphorically speaking, you are standing on top of a diving board, ready to plunge into the complex world of applied psychology to improve and develop your skills. As previously noted, the following chapters appear in no particular order of importance and you should not see them as building on top of each other. Rather, we would like you to take each one as an 'ingredient' in a recipe. It does not matter which 'ingredient' you put into the mix. You can decide how little or how much after you have read each chapter. It might be relevant to you or it might not.

The next chapter will deal with the theme of concentration. If you have experienced the feeling of suddenly 'losing focus' then Chapter 2 will help you deal with this issue.

## Short-term strategies for the here and now

This chapter has introduced the area of psychology and how it may be applied to focus on refining your skills within the classroom. Whether you have studied psychology in depth or not, it underpins every aspect of every day and being aware of psychological strategies can help professionally. The key to achieving and maintaining such success consists of:

- Focusing on the here and now as opposed to the when and then. This can keep you centred on what is important, as opposed to worrying about things that have happened or may yet happen.
- Considering what your 'ideal' teacher would look like and picturing yourself as this teacher. This can help you identify the attributes you already possess and the ones you would like to work on. Yet without picturing your future self, there is no goal to aim for.

In defining your 'ideal' teacher, it is necessary to be open and honest with yourself. By acknowledging your 'challenges', you can then take steps to overcome them. This will also help you identify the specific chapters in this book on which you may want to focus.

## Mentoring issues

You may want to discuss your reflections of this chapter with your mentor. They may be able to help you reflect on the aspects you excel at and the aspects you find challenging within your teaching, while suggesting strategies to develop.

You may also want to discuss what makes an 'ideal' teacher from their perspective: what attributes do they think are the most important for success. What challenges did they find within their teaching when they first started, and indeed, what challenges do they continue to face? By your mentor sharing these with you, you are able to acknowledge that nobody is infallible, yet by continuing to strive for perfection, you continue to improve.

## 📖 Further reading

There are many books dealing with the psychology of teaching. These fundamentally look at using psychology to facilitate the learning process. Books relating to developing personal psychological skills are more limited, however. There are a couple of books available on the market specifically aimed at teachers in relation to surviving day-to-day pressures. Both books address different issues, yet one lacks practical suggestions and the other lacks psychological underpinning.

Adams, M. (2006) *Work–Life Balance: A Practical Guide for Teachers*. London: David Fulton.
This book discusses in depth what actually impacts on the work–life balance from a theoretical perspective and provides some practical suggestions to deal with such pressures.

Allen, L. (2006) *Behind with the Marking and Plagued by Nits: Life Coaching Strategies for Busy Teachers*. Bancyfelin: Crown House.
This book provides a range of strategies for surviving teaching although the psychological underpinning behind the strategies is limited.

# 2

# What Was I Saying?
# Concentration and Attention

## Introduction

Picture the scene. Monday morning ... Your colleagues are gathering in the staffroom ready for the morning briefing, the smell of coffee and the condensation of steam on the windows cloud the accumulation of students in the playground excitedly chatting about the weekend. Your teaching plans for the week have been delivered to your line manager's desk and you have your first lesson planned and resources ready. A few notices from the headteacher, then the morning bell sounds, bringing order and uniformity to the chaos of the playground. Your students enter the room, settling quietly in anticipation of the day's events. You reach for the register as you have done so many times before … *and find it is not there.* You remember seeing it for collection in the staffroom, yet it is not in your hands. When it really matters, your attention is focused elsewhere. You somehow fail to connect your body and mind to produce the start to the week that you and the students are expecting. They sense your frustration and start to fidget and chat as you send someone to collect it and struggle to find something to discuss for this impromptu start.

Or, perhaps during a lesson a student feels sick and asks to leave the room. This throws your concentration as your lesson loses pace. It takes a while to regain focus, but by this time it is too late, the moment has passed, other students have lost concentration while you respond to the situation. If only you could switch focus again to bring the lesson back on track.

These two examples suggest that focusing attention would seem essential in successful teaching performance. Lapses in concentration or focusing attention in the wrong area of your classroom may be detrimental in the learning environment. Consequently, this chapter highlights different types of attention, the reasons for loss of focus and strategies to improve concentration.

## Chapter objectives

- Understand the elements that contribute to concentration and attentional focus.
- Consider the factors that affect attentional focus.
- Develop strategies to improve concentration and regain focus.

## Clarifying terminology

Attention and concentration are not the same, although the two terms are used interchangeably. As a result, defining concentration is not as clear as it could be. In this section, we will highlight the differences between attention, attentional focus, and concentration, so that you are clear about the link between them.

The schematic diagram (Diagram 2.1) overleaf shows how attention can be subdivided. We will use the term 'attentional focus' when referring to concentration, although either term will suffice. However, in our opinion, the term 'attentional focus' provides a form of key phrase, (similar to those discussed in Chapter 10 on self-talk) as it tells you to 'focus your attention'. The question in your mind should be, 'On what?' and you then actively

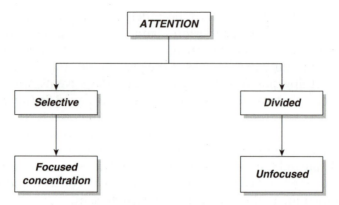

**Diagram 2.1**   A teacher's attention may initially take one of two directions (adapted from Moran, 1996)

search the environment for the relevant cues. To say 'concentrate' is perhaps too vague: it is akin to saying, 'relax' when you might not know how.

Diagram 2.1 demonstrates such 'attentional focus': to this extent, your attention may be 'selective' or 'divided'. Selective refers to focusing your concentration on one area, for example, your marking. Divided refers to the continual refocusing of your attention between competing areas. This may be, for example, engaging with your planning while watching the television. We will return to this diagram later on in the chapter.

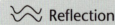 Reflection

What is your 'attentional focus' at this moment in time? Is it on reading this chapter, or is it on some other environmental stimulus (for example, the television, music, a distraction outside)? Asking yourself where your attentional focus is can help bring the mind back to the present.

 Activity 2.1

Within your teaching (and associated activities), list examples of where you are able to maintain selective attention and where your attention may be divided.

Is it always 'wrong' to have divided attention? Note down your response in your journal.

## Attention

Attention was originally defined by the psychologist, William James, over a hundred years ago, as processing 'one out of what seem several simultaneously possible objects or trains of thought ... It implies withdrawal from some things in order to deal effectively with others' (James, 1890: 403–4). This suggests that you selectively 'attend' to a single mental thought and it is this thought that goes forward in the mind. However, attention is far more than this. Despite age-old, humorous comments about the alleged 'differences' between male and female brains, the capacity of the human brain to process several pieces of information simultaneously is evident. It is also widely accepted that attention is selective, but in a more complicated way, that is, the individual is actively able to attend to relevant stimuli in the environment. Consider the times when you have overheard someone else mention your name in conversation and you have 'tuned in', as it were, to this conversation (affectionately known by psychologists as the 'cocktail phenomenon').

Of course in teaching, the importance of selective attention is no different. As you are ready for the start of a new lesson, you must filter out irrelevant information about what lessons you need to plan for tomorrow. You need to attend selectively to the students as they enter the classroom to ensure they are calm and settled, ready to learn. You must ensure that the class is ready for your first sentence in order to launch smoothly into the lesson. You must be aware of any distractions in the class that may need to be dealt with to ensure this continued flow of your teaching. If you consider the importance of selective attention during daily activities, you would have to be impressed by the way in which your brain processes information and focuses attention when working with perhaps 20–30 students at the same time. Most of your senses are providing information and your brain assembles and processes this information, before making a decision on what it believes is the best course of action (the reality of which is not always the correct course of action!).

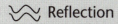 Reflection

Consider the start of a new lesson within your classroom. How do you help focus your attention? How do you help to focus the students' attention? Are there situations where you feel you may lack such selective attention? What could you do about such situations?

## Attentional focus

'Attentional focus' is the term used to describe the ability to attend to relevant information during your teaching (or indeed, any other situation requiring your attention). Environmental cues may be relevant or irrelevant to task performance. A concept called 'attentional narrowing' refers to the broadening or narrowing of this focus. In other words, attentional narrowing reduces available cues within the environment, so that cues are used, or utilized effectively. This is like the zoom function on a digital camera. One is the broad/narrow perspective, in which we take a wide or narrow view and process many, or few aspects of the environment. Within the classroom context, this is similar to working with the whole class, or a group or an individual. From time to time, your attentional focus will change to scan from the class to the individual and back. The second is the internal/external perspective, in which we view the environment either from within or outside of ourselves. We will discuss this in more detail shortly.

## Concentration

*Concentration is a prerequisite for success* within teaching. It is about being totally immersed in the here and now, in the present. The past and future are not important. Your focus on the present seems effortless. Indeed concentration and mindfulness (as discussed briefly in Chapter 1) are very similar.

There are two strategies to help keep and maintain concentration:

- *Learn to increase attention to relevant information*. This involves training yourself to focus on something specific, for example, the attention students are committing to their work, whether they are on task, and so on. However, you may first prefer to practise this with something simple, for example, focusing on a lit candle, or your breathing, for increasing periods of time.
- *Learn to decrease attention to irrelevant stimuli*. This involves training yourself to 'shut out' anything that may hinder your concentration, for example, the noise from another classroom. Again, you may prefer to practise this through a simple exercise. If you drive a car with the radio on, turn it off and try to focus ONLY on the actions of driving, each gear change, use of your mirrors, potential dangers ahead, and so on without being caught up in the music or topical discussion.

## Activity 2.2

- In relation to improving your concentration, consider each of the strategies above and how you could make these of personal relevance.
- Practise the strategies for two weeks keeping a record of how your concentration has altered.

After you have become practised in each strategy, try to use a combination of both. Filtering relevant information into conscious awareness is usually a good thing, since it is a positive attempt to increase awareness. Blocking irrelevant information from entering your mind is more risky: what may seem irrelevant at the time may in time develop into something significant. An example of this is a student not engaged with their work: they may be considering the best strategy to start their work, yet if too much time passes and they haven't started, this could indicate problems, or in turn they may start distracting others. To this extent, it may be preferable to let something irrelevant enter your mind so that you can actively evaluate and dismiss it. Think of it in terms of a Teflon™ coating on a frying pan. You can throw anything into the pan but nothing will stick, it simply washes off!

In reading the psychology literature, you will notice that concentration comprises four elements:

- Focusing selectively is necessary.
- Focus should be maintained over an undisclosed period of time.
- You should be aware of the unfolding situation.
- You should be able to alter attentional focus as required.

Lavallee et al. (2004) include an additional element for successful concentration which they call 'time sharing'. Time-sharing is simply another term for dividing your attention. In relation to teaching, you are able to divide your attention between the needs of the various students and the needs of the class in relation to your lesson plan. Another example may be in setting aside each day two hours for planning and one hour for marking as opposed to allowing this to cascade into your weekend. With this in mind, we can now develop the earlier diagram to incorporate this 'attentional shift' as demonstrated in Diagram 2.2.

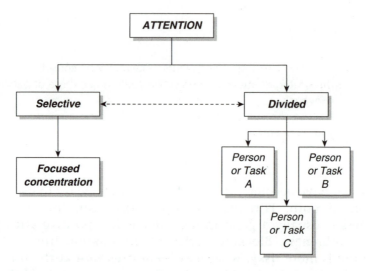

**Diagram 2.2**  Being aware of the 'attentional shift' (adapted from Lavallee et al., 2004)

 Activity 2.3

- The five elements of concentration comprise of:

  o  focusing selectively;
  o  maintaining focus;
  o  awareness of the situation;
  o  being able to alter attentional focus;
  o  sharing the time by dividing your attention to different tasks.

- For each of these elements, give yourself a score of 1 to 5 (where 1 equates to 'awful' and 5 'excellent').
- Now place these in rank order depending on the score. Put your lowest scores first.
- Keep in mind the element you want to improve.
- Periodically come back to this task over the coming weeks to reassess your development.

## Components of attention

Many theories of attention exist and to outline all of them is a topic in its own right. It is also not productive for this book. It is, however, possible for us to summarize these theories into three main categories, all of which have some relevance to teaching. Attention can be viewed as a filter, a spotlight or a resource, as we will outline below.

## Attention as a filter

You might think of attention as a filter or funnel, in which many pieces of information come into the brain, but only one of these pieces of information is processed. If you believe that *you can only concentrate on one thing at a time*, this way of thinking is relevant for you. If you do think in this way, we would ask you to consider if this was actually the case within your teaching as we are sure you can process more than a single piece of information at any given time. (Remember that teachers are supposed to 'have eyes in the back of their head'!)

## Attention as a spotlight

A different way of thinking about attentional focus is as being like the beam of a spotlight, used to pick up relevant information in a similar way to a police helicopter searching for suspects at night. You are flexible in where you 'direct the beam'. If *you are able to direct your thoughts towards specific things within the classroom*, this suggests that you are already able to focus attention. This does not mean to say that you cannot improve on using this strategy. However, it does help to identify relevant stimuli on which to focus. It also provides an explanation for what happens when you lose *concentration: focusing on the right area for too long or focusing on the wrong area*.

## Attention as a resource

A different approach to thinking about attentional focus is to campare it to a 'pool' with a limited capacity. The analogy we use with our students is of a teacup. As the tea is poured from the teapot into the cup, there is a point at which the cup will not hold any more than its capacity. If you keep pouring, tea will simply overflow and will be wasted, unless you 'empty your cup'. (Feel free to adapt this analogy to wine glass, beer glass, and so on!) In the same way, *information entering your mind will 'fill the space' until you can no longer concentrate on new information*.

Some psychologists believe that there is not one 'pool' but many pools. So, in relation to teaching, you may have a 'planning' resource pool, a 'whole-class teaching' resource pool, an 'individual support' resource pool and so on. These are not necessarily the same size, so you may be able to focus more easily on one pool because it is 'larger' than another pool. Of course, you might direct the spotlight beam, discussed above, onto one of these pools thus combining these analogies. It would be worth identifying with your mentor the types of resource pool needed for the classroom and work towards switching attentional focus between each of these at appropriate moments in time, without negatively affecting your performance.

### Activity 2.4

- Let's review the different components of attention:

  o Attention as a filter – you can only concentrate on one thing at a time.
  o Attention as a spotlight – you are able to direct your thoughts and direct the searchlight beam.
  o Attention as a resource – you are able to utilize the relevant 'pool' of resources you have at the right time.

- Consider the three different analogies above. For each of these, consider one example where you have put this into practice. For example:

  o Filter. This could relate to avoiding all distractions when marking.
  o Spotlight. This could relate to searching your mind for the relevant 'facts' you need to use when planning a lesson.
  o Resource pool. This could relate to using a specific approach to teaching an objective, phonics, scientific inquiry, and so on.

- By being aware of how you use the three components of attention, and by making these explicit, you will be able to use them to your advantage in the future.

## Different types of attentional focus

As mentioned above, your attention seems to be drawn to both relevant and irrelevant cues in the environment. Even as you read this chapter, you are probably being distracted by the noise outside, the dog, children playing, a passing car, or the ticking of the clock ... or at least you are now that we have mentioned these distractions to you! Psychologists generally agree that physiological arousal levels in the body influence whether a person will filter relevant or irrelevant cues for processing in the brain. The schematic diagram (Diagram 2.3) illustrates this nicely. Attentional input can be seen as a funnel lying on its side. Initially, all sensory information enters the funnel. Some of it is relevant (represented by a five-sided star) and some irrelevant (represented by an eight-sided star). The horizontal axis represents level of arousal and the two vertical lines represent the area of processing where relevant information is filtered in while irrelevant information is filtered out. You should notice that this happens at a moderate level of arousal. This is the essence of Easterbrook's (1959) theory: a moderate level of arousal is best for successful attentional focus. Of course, it is not quite as straightforward as

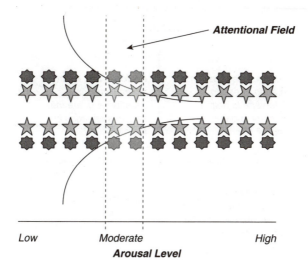

Attentional Field

Low    Moderate    High
**Arousal Level**

**Diagram 2.3**   Moderate levels of arousal should improve your attentional focus (adapted from Easterbrook, 1959)

this. You would need to establish what 'moderate' means for you, and this would undoubtedly differ from person to person.

An alternate perspective is that of Nideffer (1976) who maintains that attention can be viewed along the dimensions of direction and width. By 'direction', he means whether information is internal or external. For example, from time to time, you may adopt an *internal perspective to focus on information about how you feel*. If you are feeling tired or generally 'under the weather', you may decide to alter your teaching plans for the day to accommodate accordingly: where you may have planned to have taken a more demanding role in a physical education lesson, you may decide to change the focus to allow yourself to survive until the end of the day. In the main, however, as a teacher, you are more likely to focus on external cues, such as how the students are engaging with their work.

By 'width' Nideffer (1976) means whether to adopt a broad or narrow perspective. *A broad perspective enables you as a teacher to process various cues simultaneously*, for example, what various groups of students are engaged with. This information may allow you to make a rapid decision on which group requires support as your attentional focus is on the present. In contrast, *a narrow perspective allows a teacher to 'hone in' on one or two specific things*, for example, the next stage within the lesson, or helping a student who has encountered a difficulty.

Ultimately you will fall into one of the four quadrants as indicated in Diagram 2.4. However, you will also move around these quadrants at different times, because your brain will be processing different information as time passes. Of course, the hard part is actually moving around these quadrants at the right time! This is where the next few pages will provide you with some guidance upon what to focus.

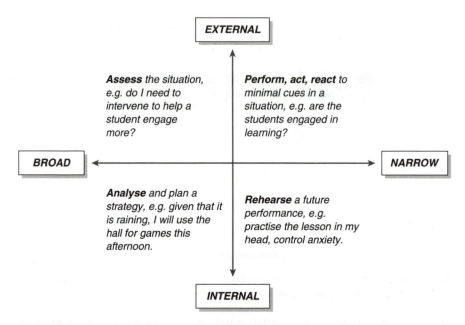

**Diagram 2.4**    Attentional focus may 'shift' depending on your needs at a specific moment in time (adapted from Nideffer, 1976)

 **Activity 2.5**

Consider the different quadrants of Diagram 2.4. Although examples have been placed in each of the quadrants, what other examples are relevant to your practice? The purpose of this activity is thus to take ownership of the model in order to identify when you may be operating in a specific quadrant.

Regardless of which quadrant you are in at any given moment, the message from this section of the chapter is very clear. Attentional focus may be adversely influenced by many potential distractions both in the environment and within yourself. It is to some of these distractions, or distractors that we shall now turn.

## Attentional distractors

As we are sure you are aware from personal experience, there are many distractions during the school day that can take your mind away from the task in hand, or divert your attention to inappropriate aspects of the environment. At a general level, these can be divided nicely into internal distractors and external distractors. One of the first things you should do, when addressing concentration problems, is to identify whether distractors are *internal or external*.

## Internal distractors

Internal distractors are, as one may expect, internalized concerns and worries about your teaching. They are thoughts and cognitions that are of little, if any, benefit to performance, and include reflecting on past events, predicting future events, panicking under pressure, fatigue and motivation.

### Reflecting on past events

Reflecting on the past is not necessarily a good thing in teaching. It is akin to superstition. 'I never enjoy teaching music.' 'I always seem to leave my planning until the last minute.' 'I can never seem to get my students to understand fractions.' Mentally this sets the mind up to do the same thing this time. It is a way of convincing yourself that the past will influence the present. Of course, having experience and knowledge are good qualities in teaching. However, they can work against you unless you use them wisely to inform your success within the classroom. In response to the quotations above, we usually *suggest that the teacher 'works in the here and now'*. Whereas we agree that reflection on past experiences is a good thing in helping to identify weaknesses and highlighting successful performances, it is not beneficial when a new term is about to begin.

### Predicting future events

'Fortune-telling' or, predicting what will happen during the current school day is also a self-induced distraction that can have adverse effects on teachers. Such distractions are relatively easy to spot, since they usually consist of 'what if' statements. For example, 'What if I have planned too much/too little to cover in the lesson?' 'What if the students seem confused?' Or even, 'What if the students don't enjoy the lesson?' By avoiding such statements and *focusing instead on the present*, on strategy and on your own and your students' performance- or process-related goals, you will not succumb to these distractions.

Another type of future-based distraction is where a thought seems to suddenly drop in to your head, such as, 'How am I going to get the students to cover all the areas before the exam?' Of course, this has nothing to do with the present lesson, but nevertheless it is an unwanted and unhelpful distraction. In Chapter 10 on self-talk, we mention using key words to regain focus. In preparing you for dealing with unwanted thoughts, we would perhaps advise you to use the word, 'STOP' as an immediate flag to show that the 'coverage' thought is a distractor. We would then help you to **substitute the distractor thought with a more appropriate replacement thought**, such as, 'I will have ensured the students fully understand the concept of this lesson'. Of course, you must practise this technique before being able to use it successfully. In the first instance, you would need to identify when thoughts of this type emerge and then to deal with them accordingly.

## Panicking, or 'choking' under pressure

We are sure that at some point in your teaching career you have succumbed to pressure; perhaps when you have been formally observed, perhaps when you have worked with a new class. Such factors may lead to panicking under pressure. Your performance suddenly drops through the floor. When it finally came to the crunch, you were unable to perform as you would have liked. Some people would argue that this is a bad thing and, yes, at one level we would have to agree. However, we would argue that if a teacher 'chokes', it is best to **take the experience, learn from it and then return even stronger than before**. From this, we would encourage you to explore your thoughts, feelings and emotions, discuss factors leading up to choking and consider how coping mechanisms can be employed to deal with the situation. Essentially, we are suggesting that choking is OK! The key is dealing with it before it happens in the future, or handling it if you suddenly feel it emerging. Nevertheless, our role is to provide a contingency plan for you to use if the situation goes too far. Choking can occur at any time and may happen when a small situation escalates to a point where several small situations are perceived as being a total catastrophe.

## Fatigue

Arguably, fatigue is more of a physical event that is beyond a teacher's control. Let's face it, if you are tired then you ARE tired! However, a consequence of fatigue may be a reduction or indeed total loss in attentional focus. **If you are able to identify fatigue as a factor in your performance, you can then deal with it appropriately**. Chapter 7 on healthy living and Chapter 9 on relaxation may provide you with strategies to overcome fatigue. Research in psychology has shown that a short, 'micro-sleep' is far more beneficial than trying to fight tiredness and keep going. We are sure you will have seen the motorway signs warning that 'tiredness kills, take a break'. While this is undoubtedly the case on the roads, thankfully this is not the case in school. However, *if you are ill-prepared you must adjust your teaching to suit the resources available to you*.

## Motivation

Motivation is key to successful teaching. If motivation levels are inadequate, attentional focus may be lost or at very least, reduced. We will discuss motivation in depth in Chapter 3. Suffice to say, for now, ***motivation helps teachers to stay focused*** on the task in hand. If you work in a school where there are highly driven teachers, the challenge will help to keep your motivation level high. If, however, you are surrounded by colleagues who no longer feel the same passion for teaching as you do, or who 'know best' as they have been teaching for years, your motivation may be reduced. Nevertheless, motivation can act as an internal distractor and this should be borne in mind if lack of attentional focus becomes an issue.

 **Activity 2.6**

- As noted above, there are a number of internal distractors:

  o Reflecting on past events;
  o Predicting future events;
  o Choking under pressure;
  o Fatigue;
  o Motivation.

- Consider an example and analyse it in the following structure:

  o Antecedent – what caused this to happen?
  o Behaviour – what did you do as a response?
  o Consequence – what happened as a result?

- Now, reconsider your response to the distractor. In light of what has been discussed, how could you have dealt with it differently? What would you expect the consequence to be?

## External distractors

External distractors, in contrast to internal distractors, are firmly located in the environment. They are provided by the sensory systems of the body. Humans have evolved as a visually dominant species and, as such, the auditory system can be a source of external distraction, both to students and teachers. An example of this is when studying or working hard on your preparation and requiring solitude, away from any noisy distractions. Furthermore, within your teaching, you may prefer just the noise from your classroom without any unwelcome, additional noise. Memories of workers fitting a new school roof while on a final teaching practice come to mind. Trying to coincide speaking in between the hammer blows was something one could not prepare for!

## Visual distractors

Visual distractors can be found everywhere and, without training to overcome them, are unavoidable. Both our offices overlook the campus road, pathway and AstroTurf beyond. There are three opportunities for visual information to compete with our attentional focus every day. Cars, pedestrians, football and hockey players use these facilities constantly, entering our field of vision and drawing our attention. We have trained ourselves to overcome this problem and instead focus on the task that we are working on at the time. Similarly, within your school, you will experience distractions in the form of other classes, lessons being conducted outside your window, unexpected visitors (governors being shown around, students from other classes) and many other distractions, all competing for your attention and inadvertently preventing you from doing your job of teaching. These factors will not change or go away. ***You should aim, therefore, to 'switch on and off' from them as you choose***. You will need to practise this. It does not just come easily. Such distractions may be different for different teachers but nevertheless, if you allow them into your attentional focus, you may have less 'space' for relevant and effective thought processes to take place.

## Auditory distractors

Schools are noisy places. Even the most calm and settled school 'hums' with residual noise. A school we experienced close to Heathrow Airport had triple glazing (and air-conditioning as the windows could never be opened due to the noise!), yet every 90 seconds, the distraction of another jet engine ascending or descending could still impact on concentration. Perhaps the class next to you is involved with a music lesson, while your class is trying to engage in a sustained writing task.

Noises not only cause the teacher to lose their concentration but also hinder the concentration of students. Even if you are able to exclude some noises, another unpredictable noise may occur.

One way to negate this is through having classical music playing in the classroom, which can help 'screen' unwanted noise while also providing a complementary auditory stimulus conducive for sustained work. This is known as the 'Mozart Effect', a term originally developed by Alfred Tomatis. There are several studies into this arguing the benefits although opinion appears divided. It wouldn't hurt, however, to give it a go as it must be better than other background noise!

## Comments from others

This category could be included with the auditory distractors, although this is where such comments may be said to affect your concentration. Whether the comments are 'throw away', disposable comments, they can sit in your mind and distract you considerably, which in turn may undermine your performance in the classroom. Such comments could include, 'I never like taking that class', 'are you sure you should be teaching … ', 'I wouldn't have done it that way', and so on. Ironically, compliments can have a similar effect. Being told how good you are at a certain aspect of teaching can cause you to think about the process, whereas before the comment you didn't need to think, you just did it.

The message here *is do not allow any comments to disrupt your attentional focus in any way, shape or form*. Be wise to what people tell you, listen to the comments, rise above them, evaluate and take them on board or dispense with them. You should be in control of what affects your performance in the classroom!

 Activity 2.7

- Make a list of external distractors.
- Consider how each of these could be negated.

   o For example, if you know when the class next door has a music lesson, could you plan your timetable for a different lesson which may require less focus from your students? Or could you negotiate with the teacher to develop a complementary timetable?
   o For visual distractors, could the classroom be structured differently? Could the windows incorporate some 'screening' (blinds, displays, and so on without losing too much natural daylight?)

- The purpose of this activity is to consider the working environment and how you can make it work for you as opposed to against you. Focusing on the ideal can set in mind what you want to achieve and how you can achieve this.
- You may similarly want to consider your home environment, making a list of aspects to help prepare your time for quality work.

## Developing, improving and refining attentional focus

So far in this chapter we have discussed what attention is and how it relates to concentration. We have introduced the idea that attentional focus is not fixed, but rather, changes as conditions dictate. It is necessary to practise techniques aimed at retaining attentional focus long before the actual event. Shifting of attentional focus is not an easy thing to do unless you have practised it beforehand.

In practising for improved concentration, you do not need to learn a new technique, beyond those described in this book. *The key lies in using the techniques we discuss in Section 3*, so we will not go into them in detail here. You may, for example, use cue words or self-talk (as detailed in Chapter 10) to provide a direction in which your attention should be guided: 'Complete my planning by 6 p.m.', or 'Be attentive to student engagement'. Alternatively, you may set process or performance goals and, in turn, evaluate these when in the classroom: that is, you are allocating resources to a particular task (see Chapter 8). You may establish so-called 'pre-performance' routines that come into play during the minutes before school starts, so that you know what you should be doing at different times; that is, you are putting the spotlight onto one or several tasks requiring your attention. Essentially, you are filling your mind up with relevant things to do, in order not to become distracted when there is seemingly nothing to do. It seems far harder to distract somebody when they are focused on something than when they are not. Try having a conversation with a friend or partner when they are engrossed in an activity. They appear not to be able to have a conversation, or if they do, it is usually minimal. (Our wives identify with this comment every time they need an answer from us when we happen to be writing!) Alternatively, you may benefit from using mental imagery as a way to avoid distractions. Practise visualizing a lesson you are to teach and gather evidence to plug into your mental image to enhance it.

In the Sport Psychology laboratory at the University of Worcester, we encourage not only athletes but groups of students from different courses to use the Batak wall. The Batak wall helps improve reaction times and consists of a set of nine lights that light up in random sequences. The participant is required to extinguish as many lights as possible and as quickly as possible in a period of time. Essentially we believe that the strengthened connections within the brain will allow people to react quicker when they need to. Why shouldn't you adopt the same principles to enhancing concentration in teaching? Indeed, tentative research on computer games may indicate that these can aid reaction times (for example, Taylor and Berry, 1998; Klicka et al., 2006) although getting the balance between playing on such games when you could be planning or marking needs to be watched! Most sporting activities would also enable you to develop your reaction times and have many additional benefits for overall health and stress reduction, as discussed in later chapters.

Combine any of these techniques to achieve your aims, but also learn to avoid 'judgemental thinking'. Judgemental thinking is the scourge of daily life. As we previously noted, teachers seem to be under the impression that they need to be judged continually, whether this is their self-reflection or through numerous lesson observations. The end result is usually negative and adversely influences future performance. For example, if you have made a mistake in one lesson, it does not mean that that you should reflect on that error for the remainder of the day: if you do, your performance will be poor. ***Deal with the mistake, evaluate it quickly, and then move on***. It has happened, you can do nothing about it but you can change how you tackle the same issue next time around. ***A mistake is not a mistake if you learn from it***. Experience comes from making mistakes as this allows you to acquire experience. We would be the first to acknowledge our mistakes yet each one has improved our performance.

## Mindfulness

As noted in Chapter 1, mindfulness is keeping in the present moment, keeping your attention focused solely on what you are doing … here … now. It is being aware of and paying full attention to the moment, letting thoughts come and go without engaging with them, just observing them. The past or future are of no concern. For example, are you reading this book or has your mind 'wandered'? No doubt you have not been thinking about a black cat, until these two words have been mentioned. In your mind is a black cat – how long will that image be held while you continue reading? Or have you 'forgotten' about it and are now attending to how this sentence will finish?

Although mindfulness may be traced back to Eastern contemplative traditions (for example, in Buddhism and other meditative practices) mindfulness is currently undergoing a surge in popularity due to the work of Jon Kabat-Zinn (among others) to help deal with psychological and physical conditions. The paradoxical debate occurs whether a person can be in a full state of mindfulness, as being so, you would not need to train in it – you would be completely lost in the moment without realizing you were trying to bring about the 'state'. Yet, mindfulness training is acknowledged as a way of focusing (and relaxing) the mind and body.

Mindfulness may be practised in any everyday engagement. The example above is whether you are 'mindfully' reading this paragraph. How does the book feel in your hands? How are you sitting? Is the chair becoming too hard? Are your muscles feeling tired from sitting in this position? How does your intention move your eyes across the page? How are the words processed in your mind? How are the concepts forming in your mind? Indeed, being fully aware, or mindful, of the 'event' and the actions and processes involved is the essence of mindfulness.

**Activity 2.8**

Mindfulness may be practised at any time as discussed above with the example of reading this book. To this extent, being aware of all your senses involved in the process can help facilitate mindfulness.

Consider mindfulness the next time you eat:

- What are each of your senses telling you at this moment about the food ... the smell, the look, the taste, the texture, the colour.
- What physical movements are involved in the process of eating? Reaching for the food, perhaps cutting it, lifting it to your mouth, and so on.
- Are you mindfully eating, or are you watching the television while you eat? Are you focused on biting then chewing each mouthful? Or are you just 'wolfing' it down?
- How do your teeth feel as you bite/chew? What flavour is released into your mouth? How does your jaw move, your tongue?
- Can you track the food as you swallow?
- At what point do you feel 'full'?

Consider when else you could practise mindfulness, for example, when walking, driving, speaking, breathing ... make the intention to 'mindfully' engage once a day with an activity.

## One-minute summary

Attention and concentration are crucial to effective performance. If a teacher is not competent in switching attention, focusing and refocusing when things go awry, this can cause loss of focus and in turn create a variety of problems.

Concentration consists of the following elements:

- focusing selectively;
- maintaining focus over a period of time;
- awareness of the situation as it develops;
- being able to alter attentional focus;
- sharing the time by dividing your attention to different tasks.

If any of these elements are not synchronized, then you may have difficulty. The key is to ensure you are aware which element is not working well in order to address it.

There are several attentional distractors which may be external (for example, noise) or internal (for example, motivation or reflecting on past events). Again, it is necessary to identify the distractor in order to deal with it. Ultimately, the key to success is being able to maintain attention and this can be trained specifically through increasing attention to relevant information while decreasing attention to irrelevant information. The various chapters in this book will unite to help develop attentional focus, specifically those outlined in Section 3.

Being 'mindful' can certainly help aid your concentration, along with promoting relaxation (Chapter 9) and reducing stress (Chapter 5).

## Short-term strategies for the here and now

- Limit as many distractors as possible. (Of course the key is to identify what the distractor is in the first place.)
- Try this sequence:

  o Keep focused on the present moment, on what you are doing.
  o If you find your attention wandering, STOP.
  o Close your eyes.
  o Focus on your breathing completely.
  o Count nine breaths concentrating fully on the breathing process.
  o Next, say in your mind what you will focus on when you open your eyes.
  o Back this up verbally with an intention 'I will continue my marking'.

- Although this process may take a couple of minutes, in the long run it will save you time on the task you are engaged with.
- If, however, you need to bring your attention to the present within the classroom context:

  o Focus on taking a few breaths.
  o Close your eyes momentarily (a second may be long enough): this will signal that you have stopped and will refocus when you open your eyes again.
  o Mentally say the phrase 'bring your focus back to the NOW', 'be HERE, NOW' or something equivalent.
  o Open your eyes.

- Be mindful!

## Mentoring issues

One of the tasks previously noted is that you may want to consider with your mentor the different 'resource pools' required for success within the classroom.

You may also want to discuss whether they perceive you lack attentional focus within any part of your lesson. (Observers can sometimes hone in on some aspect you may be totally unaware of!) Furthermore, you may want to discuss how attentional distractors could be limited.

## Further reading

As with most of the chapters in this book, guidance and strategies in one area may well impact on another. Although the benefits of meditation (or concentrating on one thing, if you prefer not to have any esoteric connotations!) will be discussed further in this book, any resources that enable such meditation will be of benefit: the key is finding one that you feel happy with.

There are limited resources available for improving concentration and attention. However, the following would be worth looking at:

Bruce, B. (2003) *Mental Aerobics: 75 Ways to Keep Your Brain Fit*. Nashville, TN: Abingdon Press.
The book provides exercises for mental agility including developing focus and concentration.

Horn, S. (1995) *Concentration! How to Focus for Success*. Menlo Park, CA: Crisp Publications.
Although this is a relatively short book (and quite dated now!) it provides a series of exercises to develop mental discipline and to remain focused while also being able to prioritize.

An academic reference focusing on concentration and attention that may be applied to the teaching context is:

Nideffer, R.M. and Sagal, M.S. (2006) 'Concentration and attention control training', in J.M. Williams (ed.), *Applied Sport Psychology: Personal Growth to Peak Performance*. 5th edn. Mountain View, CA: Mayfield.

A couple of studies into the 'Mozart Effect' are also listed here, should you wish to examine this further, although further searching of academic databases will provide additional resources.

Thompson, W.F., Schellenberg, E.G. and Husain, G. (2002) 'Arousal, mood, and the Mozart Effect', *Psychological Science*, 12(3): 248–51.

Wilson, T. and Brown, T. (1997) 'Re-examination of the effect of Mozart's music on spatial task performance', *Journal of Psychology*, 131(4): 365.

# What Am I Doing Here?
# Motivation

## Introduction

Motivation is an extremely complex psychological process that can enable teachers to excel and thrive in the classroom, in turn ensuring their students similarly achieve such high standards. However, a lack of motivation may be blamed when a teacher's performance drops below 'acceptable' levels. A teacher may benefit from direct words by their line manager or the headteacher so that they return to performing their duties appropriately. Yet for some teachers, this type of action may do more harm than good and can lead to even worse performance in the classroom. Consider the variety of students you work with: some may be motivated by a few words, yet others may require a complex mix of strategies. So, how do you know what works for you? In this chapter, we will explore some of the issues around the complex nature of motivation and provide some guidance on what to consider when motivating yourself or others.

## Chapter objectives

- Define the concept of motivation and how it applies to teachers.
- Understand different motivational influences.
- Appreciate the role of appropriate feedback.
- Apply motivational strategies in order to develop your motivation.

## What exactly is 'motivation'?

As noted in the introduction, motivation is complex. There are numerous theories and perspectives on the subject and the chapter here will do little justice to the area! If motivation is such a complex concept, it is little surprise to discover that defining it is not easy. However, for operational purposes, there are several ways of considering motivation. At a very general level, motivation is a state that drives us to act in a certain way. As authors, we are motivated to finish writing this chapter in a clear, explicit manner to engage the reader while covering a number of strategies. But if you put any 'excuse' to do something less work related in front of us, we won't even reach the end of this …

Our motivation will have changed. Some people see motivation as little more than a physiological state of arousal. The more aroused or 'psyched up' you are, the greater your motivation to achieve or perform your teaching role. Yet, as we pointed out in Chapter 2, if you are too aroused, your level of concentration will drop and your performance will dip. If this happens, we guarantee your dip in motivation won't be far behind!

Similarly, if you are feeling extremely tired, lethargic and lacking in energy (a low state of physiological arousal), the last thing you may want to do is stand in front of a class of students and facilitate a wondrous learning experience. If on the other hand, you feel full of energy, you would probably relish the thought of engaging with such a session. Similarly, if everything is going well psychologically speaking, you are more likely to want to continue providing this same high-quality learning experience, where you find you are being paid for a job you love doing.

Nevertheless, motivation is far more than either of these. It is based on several extra psychological factors such as how highly you value your goals; your expectations; and possible conflicting motives. Psychologists differentiate between external and internal motivation, and these are important to the way teachers think about their teaching.

## External or 'extrinsic' motivation

Extrinsic motivation is the term given to those people who teach for external reasons. *Your motivation comes from rewards or from other people*. Ask yourself the question, 'Why do I teach?' The question is trying to discover whether you teach for rewards such as the financial gain, long holidays, and so on. We are, however, guessing that it may be for other reasons than these!

If you teach for extrinsic reasons, you will be spurred on by reward and, as long as you continue in a rich vein of good form, the rewards will continue. However, when things go less successfully, you will experience the flip side of reward, punishment, such as being harsh on yourself or others commenting on your poor performance. The consequences of such performances are usually negative and, although punishment may give you the 'kick up the backside' to get back on track, it is arguably among the best demotivating practice you can experience. Moreover, *rewards also begin to lose their reinforcing nature after a while and you will need greater rewards to satisfy the drive to succeed*. Viewed in this way, rewards are rather like addictions, whereby the 'hit' needs to be more intense to gain the same amount of pleasure previously experienced.

## Internal or 'intrinsic' motivation

In contrast, *intrinsic motivation comes from within*. It is about fulfilment and satisfaction or the desire to 'get it right'. In working with a teacher, we would ask the question, 'If all the holidays and high pay were taken away, would you still teach?' If the answer is, 'Yes', we would be pleased that you are teaching for the best reasons. *Among the hardest things we have to do, is ask teachers NOT to teach for such extrinsic rewards*. They usually look at us with total bewilderment: 'Are they asking me to teach for free?' Instead, we are asking you to place emphasis on mastering your own teaching so that it is this that provides satisfaction and fulfilment. ***Be a teacher to teach: focus on the process of teaching***.

If you consider the process of how to put in a satisfying teaching experience, rather than considering the outcome, you will have a far better chance of enjoying your teaching. So if you teach for intrinsic reasons, the holidays and financial remuneration are likely to come as a 'side effect' or consequence of your intrinsic reasons for teaching, which is to be the best teacher you can be.

Having understood the difference between intrinsic and extrinsic motivation, there is one additional comment to make at this point. It is not wholly 'wrong' to be extrinsically motivated. The key is to have an element of extrinsic motivation alongside an element of intrinsic motivation. In this way, you will gain pleasure from both. Let's face it, being given a bottle of wine by the headteacher for arranging the school sports day is always a nice feeling!

 Activity 3.1

- In your journal list what motivated you to enter the teaching profession. Were these intrinsic or extrinsic motivators?
- Consider your motivation for teaching now. Are these intrinsic or extrinsic motivators?
- Compare your prior and present reasons for teaching. Have these changed? If so, why?

## Some theories of motivation

One way to look at motivation is rather like a ***drive or urge, pushing us to achieve our best***. When the drive diminishes, motivation is lost. Motivation may therefore be related to physiological arousal. If the body is sufficiently aroused (physiologically speaking, not explicitly speaking!), levels of motivation remain high. However, motivation may also be viewed in terms of part of our personality, a ***personality trait***. We might describe you as a highly motivated person, suggesting that you are motivated in many aspects of your life, not just in teaching.

You may have previously come across the following theory in your teacher training: Maslow's (1970) 'Hierarchy of Needs' is widely covered in education as conceptually it makes sense, despite the model being dated and criticized.

In Diagram 3.1, motivation drives us to move through each stage of the pyramid until we reach the top. At the bottom of the pyramid, our priority is to satisfy basic survival needs and desires, such as obtaining

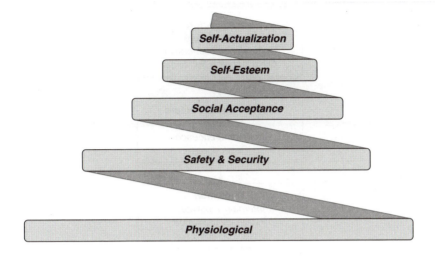

**Diagram 3.1**   Maslow's 'Hierarchy of Motivation' (adapted from Daniels, 2005)

food. We are then motivated to find shelter, before seeking approval from others and approval from ourselves until we reach the pinnacle of mastery that he termed 'self-actualization'. Self-actualization is synonymous with the best you can be: it is the place where a teacher finds everything almost effortless. An hour-long lesson seems like it is over in minutes, the day passes effortlessly.

Taking this idea further, people are motivated towards achieving competence and mastery in all areas of their lives. Attempts to master different circumstances help us to feel good about our ability as teachers: this may manifest as tackling a concept you find difficult explaining in a new way, refreshing your knowledge about an area, considering a new teaching approach you have not previously considered, and so on. *You will seek out challenges to 'prove' your capability and personal competence*.

In contrast, if your attempts at mastery result in failure, your motivation will decrease and the negative, downward spiral of despair will emerge. The message for teachers is clear: *do not underestimate your personal competence. If you do, you are likely to prefer activities that fail to 'stretch' you and you will ultimately lose the motivation to continue teaching*. It is also important to pay attention to your feelings about your attempts at mastery. Regardless of whether you are successful in your attempt, does it make you feel positive or negative? If your performance is poor, it is not necessarily a good sign to be overly critical as this will combine with your negative feelings and help to demotivate you. Rather, you should reflect on why your performance was unsatisfactory and what the solution is to the challenge.

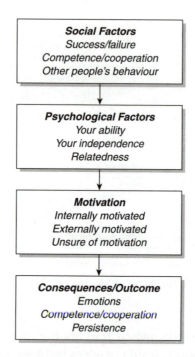

**Diagram 3.2**   Components that impact on motivation (adapted from Vallerand, 2001)

## What factors influence motivation?

According to the schematic diagram (Diagram 3.2), there are four components that make up our motivation in teaching: social factors, psychological mediators, underlying motivation and perceived outcomes. We will cover each of these in turn to build a usable picture for teachers.

## Social factors

Social factors play such an important role in motivating teachers. The need to achieve success is motivating in itself. However, you may adopt the opposite position, being motivated instead to avoid failure. We would always ask you to think differently about success and failure. Negativity should be pounced on and discarded. *The behaviour of other people in the staffroom will undoubtedly influence your own behaviour and, ultimately, your motivation.*

You might consider observing and evaluating how other staff members function around you, what issues emerge and how you deal with them. For example, because you may be relatively new to the profession, do other members of staff listen to and respect your ideas equally alongside the views of longer-serving teachers? We have known this to be the case and this has affected teacher's motivation because of the apparent lack of fairness.

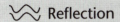 **Reflection**

- Consider your working situation at the moment.
- Are there any people you work with who 'ooze' positive energy?
- Are there any people you work with who always seem to be negative?
- Consider what you could do when someone starts talking negatively. Can you counter with a positive comment? Can you change the situation or remove yourself from the situation? Can you consider a positive affirmation mentally? (See Chapter 10.)

## Psychological mediators

Social factors inevitably influence a teacher's psychological state. It is not necessarily the reality of those social factors that is significant, but rather, your perception of the situation. The perception of your competence comes partly from social factors. We discuss issues relating to self-confidence further in the next chapter. Suffice to say, *if you have a poor perception of your competence, this will undoubtedly influence your motivational states in a negative way*. Ideally, you should strive for autonomy or independence.

By controlling how you improve the way that you teach, you will be teaching for intrinsic or internal reasons rather than external rewards. The danger in teaching for external rewards is that if they were taken away, perhaps due to poor performance, then levels of motivation would also inevitably diminish. Our advice would perhaps focus on helping you to enhance your perceptions of competence and autonomy by offering guidance on identifying the positives that show that you are capable and could 'do this with your eyes shut' (metaphorically speaking, of course).

## Underlying motivation

We discussed intrinsic and extrinsic motivation at the beginning of this chapter. In terms of the flow diagram, however, social and psychological factors influence a teacher's motivation to varying degrees and this is linked to the type of motivation they hold. Of course, if you consider that you are an extrinsically motivated person, then our role would perhaps involve trying to assist you in moving towards a more intrinsic focus, so that the potential pitfalls are fewer and possibly easier to overcome. If a teacher is amotivated, this means that they show no real preference. It does not mean that you have no motivation. Instead it means that you have lost sight of why you teach. Amotivation might indicate a slide towards a teacher quitting the profession. Ask yourself the question again, 'Why do I teach?' *If you don't know what motivates you, how can you set goals, achieve those goals and progress beyond them?* If you are unable to answer this question, don't panic. The simple solution is to start setting goals for yourself so that you can get back on track to successful teaching. Indeed, Chapter 8 discusses goal setting in detail.

## Consequences/outcomes

Now we arrive at perhaps the most important aspect of motivation, the outcome or consequence of your behaviour. *If social factors and perceptions are positive and intrinsic motivation is high, there is a good likelihood that outcomes will also be positive.* Emotions are likely to be positive. If you have had a good lesson, you might feel elated. This feeling plugs directly back into your feedback mechanism, telling your brain that you are competent, you are in control and you can pull out all the stops when you need to. *Positive emotion is a way of telling the rational, cognitive part of your brain that things feel good.*

This is vital for us because we believe that the key to successful performance lies in the process and how it feels, rather than the outcome. If you feel 'good' about your performance, issues of poor performance, anxiety, self-confidence, comments from others, negativity from other teachers, and so on will not detract, or indeed distract you from achieving your goals in the classroom. You will be more inclined to brush these things aside, in the knowledge that, 'Despite these minor irritations, I can still do the business'. Those teachers who can be heard vociferously berating others for their actions are already beginning to direct their motivation in the wrong place. Look around at the staff meeting and you will be able to identify this type of behaviour.

*Highly motivated teachers are more likely to be persistent.* Nothing will stop them from achieving their goals.

 ### Activity 3.2

What makes you feel 'good' about your teaching? What indicators demonstrate to you that you have facilitated a good lesson? Make a note of these in your journal.

## The brain's 'chemical high'

It is important to point out that you may receive a physiological 'high' rather like an addictive reward for successful performances in the class-room. Having received this reward (or elevation of dopamine levels in the brain) you are more likely to strive to seek out the pleasurable sensation again and again. This is perhaps why sexual desires are so strong in humankind. *This physiological change in brain chemistry is in itself a highly motivating experience and is one that helps to maintain motivational levels*, *only* for as long as it continues to be experienced. As discussed earlier, we would not suggest that your only reason for teaching should be to satisfy potentially addictive cravings, but it does offer a satisfying feeling when you can get it! There is little else as satisfying as the feeling associated with a successful lesson.

Psychologically, the 'chemical high' can be compared to Csikszentmihalyi's (pronounced chick-sent-me-hal-yi) (2000, 2008) notion of 'flow', whereby it seems that you act spontaneously and effortlessly, being fully absorbed in the moment, in full control and where time seems to transform (either time can stand still or speed up). Such a flow state can similarly be addictive, where you may try to achieve that moment time and again within your teaching. (We will discuss the state of 'flow' in greater detail in the final chapter.)

## Developing motivation

Based on the motivation literature, a useful set of guidelines for teachers emerges to assist in building motivation. We will interpret these guidelines (adapted from Weinberg and Gould, 2007) and deal with each below.

## Situational and personal factors in motivation

Personal factors interact with the situation teachers find themselves in. For example, you may have been observed by a mentor and the lesson didn't go particularly well so you don't relish the thought of your next observation. On the other hand, you may have had a very successful observation and are therefore highly motivated to do well again. Alternatively, the class hamster may have died and this has left you upset and traumatized (tongue firmly pressed in cheek).

Consequently, *it is important to establish how much these factors are influencing your motivation levels*. Your progress is only possible if you have a strong foundation. In exploring situational and personal factors, it is possible to create this foundation.

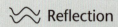 Reflection

Are there any factors currently that are constraining your performance in the classroom? Can any of these be resolved? Consider other strategies in this book for example, Chapter 4: Confidence and self-esteem, Chapter 5: Emotion, mood and stress, Chapter 8: Goal setting.

## Appropriate feedback in motivation

It is important for teachers to be provided with appropriate feedback, when reflecting on their performances. Whether this comes from a tutor, a mentor or even your own perspective, the feedback needs to be appropriate. This links directly with the way in which people assess their performance. If a teacher is not performing optimally, perhaps as a result of illness, they should not expect to perform as well as when they are in peak condition. Yet, time and time again we hear the despair in their voices because they are attributing their 'less than successful' performance to lack of ability when physical condition is the culprit. The next time you have a cold, for example, assess your journey on the way to school. You will not feel as 'alive' as when you are 100 per cent fit. So why should it be any different when you are teaching after an illness or injury? It is important therefore, to monitor whether you are assessing your performance appropriately in light of these judgements and correct any misperceptions.

## Perceived competence or ability and motivation

Appropriate feedback is an important way of influencing your perceived competence. If a teacher monitors and reflects on his or her performances, searching for and picking out positive information, they will feel a heightened sense of competence: 'I can do this, because I am a successful teacher.' This becomes self-perpetuating, feeding back into itself rather like a loop. *Competence leads to positive thoughts about your performance, which leads to a feeling of competence*, which leads to positive thoughts about your performance, which leads to competence, and so on. If you are competent, you are more likely to be in control of the situation and your motivation will remain high.

## Process goals in motivation

As we have pointed out elsewhere in this and other chapters, focusing on the outcome is not necessarily the best approach to adopt. Process or mastery of the task is, in our opinion more important. If a teacher can master their profession and set out to achieve the best they can in the classroom, they should have an enjoyable and successful teaching career. In a way, this is more productive than trying to ensure students pass exams and make the grade as it is not possible to exert control over all aspects of learning: *we can only influence learning*. If the teacher focuses on mastery of performance instead of outcome, then, the teacher is teaching to the best of their ability and students will naturally engage with the learning process and as such, become driven to succeed.

Professor Joan Duda, an expert in motivation, from the University of Birmingham, UK, suggests that people can enhance their level of involvement in a task in a number of ways. These can be adopted in teaching and we have adapted some of them in Table 3.1. You may use these strategies when thinking about ways to increase your level of motivation in teaching.

**Table 3.1**   Strategies to increase motivation

| What is the situation? (Situational structure) | What should I do about it? (Strategies) |
| --- | --- |
| I am finding it difficult to achieve (Task attainment) | Use SMART(ER) goal setting<br>Make the demands of the task individualized and specific<br>Discuss with mentor your progress and your goals |
| I am unsure about how much control I have in what happens (Authority) | Teacher to take responsibility for own professional development<br>Teacher to be actively involved in decision-making process<br>Discuss with mentor the issue of autonomy: what needs to be covered, what would be good to cover, what can be left |
| I am not being given accurate and honest recognition for my achievement (Recognition) | Recognize individual progression and effort<br>Ask mentor for an appraisal |
| I don't know whether I am making progress or whether my standard of teaching is acceptable (Evaluation and standards) | Develop evaluation criteria related to goals set<br>Set own self-evaluation schedule<br>Ensure consistency and meaningfulness<br>Ask mentor for an observation and to review planning/marking, etc. |
| I am expected to deliver when preparation has been limited (Appropriateness of timing) | Provide adequate time for future preparation<br>Consider reviewing the working week to capitalize on time available<br>Discuss with mentor any schemes/resources available to aid planning |

**Activity 3.3**

- Consider the situational factors listed above.
- For each of these elements, give yourself a score of 1 to 5 (where 1 equates to 'awful' and 5 'excellent').
- Place these in rank order depending on the score. Put your lowest score(s) first.
- Keep in mind the situational factor you want to improve.
- Periodically come back to this task over the coming weeks to reassess your development.

## Self-determination theory

Many of the aspects discussed above are encompassed in what is known as 'self-determination theory' (SDT). Edward Deci and Richard Ryan (1985) have been fundamental in evolving this theory, which asserts that individuals are motivated if they:

- Feel *competent* in controlling their environment and are able to predict outcomes of their actions.
- Feel *autonomous* in that they can determine their own course of action without interference from others.
- Feel *relatedness* which refers to satisfactory engagement with others in the social world.

If all three are in order, the individual can 'grow' through taking control of personal challenges. An example of SDT in action is considering a teacher who is able to discuss their planning with others and feels that they have been able to discuss honestly and openly about the subject content for a particular theme in the year group's planning (relatedness). From this, they have the freedom to decide how best to put the planning into action (autonomy). Finally, they have the skills and ability to ensure that the lessons capitalize on their personal strengths while engaging the students in a stimulating manner (competence).

 **Activity 3.4**

A number of psychological measures have been developed in relation to SDT. They may be found at: www.psych.rochester.edu/SDT/index.html.

The following statements have been derived from one such scale:

|   |   | Yes/No |
|---|---|---|
| 1 | I often feel free to make decisions about my students. | |
| 2 | I often feel a valued member of the staff. | |
| 3 | I often understand how my emotions affect me in the classroom. | |
| 4 | I often feel that my professional accomplishments are due to my own doing. | |
| 5 | I often feel that I can be myself in the classroom. | |
| 6 | I am often aware of how my body feels and how this affects my teaching. | |
| 7 | I often have a choice in decisions that influence my classroom practice. | |
| 8 | I often have the freedom to make my own decisions about my classroom practice. | |
| 9 | I often feel that I have the ability to teach to the best of my abilities. | |
| 10 | I often feel in control of my classroom. | |

No doubt, if you have answered the above statements positively, you are likely to have a higher self-determined nature in relation to your practice.

If, however, your responses have been rather more negative, you may want to discuss this with your mentor in order to identify how you can feel more in control.

## One-minute summary

We have introduced the concept of motivation as being vital to all areas of one's life, especially teaching. Without motivation, you would fail miserably. Without motivation, there would be little reason to get out of bed in the morning for work. However, at some point, many if not all of us experience dips in motivation, which, if left unattended grow increasingly larger and more distinct. *When motivation is high, nothing stops us*. We set out to do something and we strive towards achieving that goal. The goal itself should be carefully devised and should, we would argue, to be related to mastery of a task rather than its outcome. Strategies can be put in place to ensure that motivation levels are established or retained and control over situational and personal factors will help to do this. Motivation is linked nicely with self-confidence and self-esteem, the focus of Chapter 4.

## Short-term strategies for the here and now

- Consider your level of motivation in general for teaching.
- Note down the intrinsic and extrinsic motivators that drive you. Ensure you make your list of intrinsic motivators longer than the extrinsic.
- Consider factors that may be influencing your motivation negatively. Develop strategies to avoid such factors (for example, keeping away from colleagues who seem to drain you).
- Reward yourself with an activity or treat for your teaching periodically. This could be taking part in a hobby, sport, and so on, something that indicates a definite 'cut off' point from your teaching.

## Mentoring issues

Activity 3.3 would be worth considering with your mentor in terms of the situational factors that may be impacting on your motivation. It would be worth sharing your results from the exercise with them. You may also want to discuss issues about self-determination and how your feelings of autonomy, competence and relatedness can be encompassed.

It would also be worth exploring your mentor's motivational resources – what drives them when they feel below par? What strategies do they use?

## 📖 Further reading

There are literally hundreds of resources relating to motivation: finding one which helps develop your motivation can be like looking for the proverbial needle in a haystack ... be warned!

In terms of academic content, the following would be worth looking at:

Reeve, J.M. (2008) *Understanding Motivation and Emotion.* 5th edn. Chichester: John Wiley and Sons.
This book is what we deem as one of the ultimate, encompassing works on motivation, discussing the wide range of theoretical perspectives that influence motivation.

The Self-Determination Theory website (www.psych.rochester.edu/SDT/) has a number of resources and publications available for download.
Some of the self-help books are listed here:

Burn, G. (2008) *Motivation for Dummies*. Chichester: John Wiley and Sons.
Yet another 'for Dummies' book. We wish we were on commission for the number of books that we recommend. Put simply, however, these books are well-written, clearly structured, with some very useful suggestions and value for money.

Chandler, S. (2004) *100 Ways to Motivate Yourself: Change Your Life Forever.*
   Franklin Lakes, NJ: Career Press.
A very positive book with numerous suggestions that are practical and relevant.

Vendera, J.J., Burnside, M. and Guerville, B. (2008) *Mindset: Programming Your Mind For Success*. USA: The Voice Connection/Vendera Publishing.
This book takes a practical approach as it guides you through the chapters and activities, encouraging you to keep a journal for your reflections.

# I Can't Do It! Confidence and Self-esteem

# Introduction

Self-confidence is that elusive, magical ingredient that gives us supremacy over our thoughts, actions and, ultimately, our performances. When self-confidence is high, it seems that nobody else can teach as effectively as us. In contrast, when self-confidence is low our teaching world seems to fall apart. Everything seems to go wrong. Everybody else seems so much 'better' than we are. As we explain in Chapter 5 on emotion, mood and stress, this leads to a damaging, downward spiral that is perceived as irretrievable. All it takes, however, is that one lesson where things pick up and self-confidence starts to return. In this chapter, we shall explain the elements that contribute to self-confidence, provide ways of identifying the symptoms associated with low self-confidence and provide guidance on overcoming the situation.

# Chapter objectives

- Define self-confidence in terms of how it relates to your classroom practice.
- Understand why self-confidence is situation specific.
- Identify symptoms that indicate low self-confidence.
- Develop strategies for developing self-confidence.

# What is self-confidence?

Self-confidence is a difficult concept to define. It is an expectation about achieving success. It should, however, be a realistic expectation. Overconfidence in a teacher's ability can be as damaging as lack of confidence. The key is finding your own peak and staying there for as long as possible. So, self-confidence is not something that one either has or does not have. We all have a certain level of self-confidence all of the time, which we may need to increase or reduce to arrive at an optimal level for performance.

Self-confidence can be viewed in two ways. You might be a confident person in all kinds of situations, whether this is in the classroom, in your career, or in your social life.

Alternatively, you might be a confident person in particular situations and not in others. For example, if you are confident in teaching second year students and then decide, or are allocated to teach a different year group, you may find that your confidence falls away as you stand in the classroom on the first day of the autumn term (something that is not uncommon for many teachers). The specific situation is causing you to doubt yourself and your confidence goes down as a result.

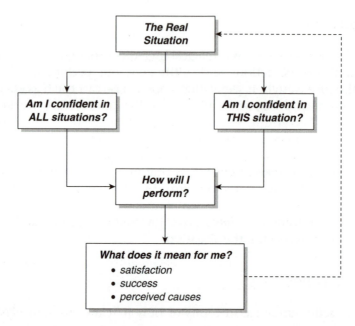

**Diagram 4.1**    Perceiving the reality of a situation (adapted from Vealey, 1986)

The schematic diagram (Diagram 4.1) provides a useful framework for us to explain how self-confidence may affect a teacher mentally. The extent to which teachers believe in their ability to be successful is the key to this diagram.

Different teachers perceive the reality of a situation in different ways. It is how we interpret the signals of a situation that is important. The classroom remains the same; the curriculum generally stays the same, and so on. The teacher brings to the lesson his or her general level of self-confidence and attitude to teaching ('Am I confident in all situations?'). This is complemented by the teacher's level of self-confidence for the particular lesson at this moment in time. It might be the case that you are confident in all situations but find that you are suddenly not feeling confident *now*. Alternatively, it might be that you are not generally a confident person, but today you are feeling so good and so confident that nothing can stop you. So, ask yourself the question, 'Am I confident in *this* situation?' How you answer this question will have an influence on how well you perform in the classroom.

Your actual performance may be positive or negative depending on how confident you are up to the start of the lesson. The 'killer blow' to self-confidence is dealt with when you ask the question, 'What does it mean for me?' Humans simply love to compare themselves with and evaluate themselves against others or their previous performance. The tools we use to evaluate ourselves are success, satisfaction and perceived causes of failure.

A teacher's perception of success is usually driven by outcomes: 'If the lesson didn't go well, I failed.' Satisfaction is linked closely with success: 'I am not satisfied because not all students achieved the learning outcomes.' As we point out throughout this book, neither of these thoughts is very productive or indeed even appropriate and we would challenge teachers to question them. Yes, successful teaching is important. Of course it is, otherwise why are we following this career? Nevertheless, success and satisfaction feed back into our self-confidence and fuel it, or destroy it, for the next lesson. How many times has your second lesson gone 'pear-shaped' because you lost confidence after the first lesson? There are better ways of using psychology to help your teaching rather than using it to hinder you. After your first lesson, look at the possible reasons for your performance and we do mean reasons *not* excuses! If it was a good performance, you will focus on the positives, take the glory and move forward with heightened self-confidence.

However, if it was a poor performance, you probably look for and magnify the negatives, while ignoring or minimizing the positives. This will more than likely lead to feelings of negativity and may cause you to question your own ability. How irrational can this be? You have improved from your early days in teaching, or from your first teaching placement. You have the potential, the capability, the skills, the motivation and everything else that constitutes a successful teacher. Yet, here you are questioning yourself when you should be focusing on *how* to achieve your goals. Once self-confidence takes a dive, it is difficult, although not insurmountable, to retrieve it. So, if you have a 'poor' performance you should also look for the positives, however small these may appear to be.

Overconfidence is equally harmful. Overconfidence occurs when a teacher's confidence does not match the reality of their capabilities. If you do not possess the skills to do the things you believe you can do, you *will* fail. Of course, this is not to say that you may be unable to achieve a respectable level of competence at some point in the future, just not in the here and now. Overconfidence tends not to last too long, since the reality of constantly performing poorly will tug at the conscience of even the thickest-skinned person.

Lack of self-confidence is sometimes disguised, so that the 'outside world' is not aware of the true situation. For example, a teacher who lacks self-confidence may compensate by 'acting' in a confident manner. This false confidence usually manifests itself as arrogance and pretentiousness but is in fact a form of overconfidence. Returning to our earlier comment about perceiving situations realistically, the teacher who experiences false confidence is misinterpreting the signs from the situation and needs to refocus his or her efforts to 'tune in' to the right signs, the signs that will provide solutions.

### Activity 4.1

- Divide a page in two. On one side, list three aspects that you are confident about within your role. On the other side, list three aspects that you feel you could develop your confidence with.
- What do you consider to be the success indicators of the aspects you are confident about?
  - For example, if I was confident about time management, the success indicators may be that my planning and resources are always ready on time, that I allow time for delays on my way to school, that I have a timely pace to my lessons.
- What do you consider to be the success indicators of those aspects you feel less confident about? Consider the positive attributes you already have within this aspect.
  - For example, if I did not feel too confident about behaviour management, what would I expect to see if I did feel confident? Possible answers could include that all students remained on task when working individually.
  - I could then note down the positive attributes within behaviour management, for example, I am able to gain and keep everyone's attention when introducing the lesson, that students do complete the set tasks, and so on.
- Completing this activity will help you identify the key issues which may act as barriers to your confidence. Furthermore, this activity will help you identify specifically what you may be able to focus on to ensure you can strive to gain confidence in this area.

## Strategies for enhancing self-confidence

If a teacher's self-confidence is underdeveloped or has deteriorated, it is necessary to raise or restore it. The first consideration would be to reflect your self-confidence in specific situations. The psychologist, Albert Bandura (1977), talks about self-confidence in specific situations and suggests that we look at four related elements: performance accomplishments, vicarious experience, verbal persuasion, and physiological arousal. We will show below how each one relates to teaching.

## Performance accomplishments: assess your performance

Capability is partially determined by previous accomplishments. Self-confidence is increased if previous performances were successful.

It suggests that mastery of teaching skills is taking place and progress is being made. In contrast, self-confidence is reduced if previous accomplishments have been poor. You should identify even the smallest improvements within the school day. By doing this, you will elevate its importance in your mind and will feel good. For example, if you have accomplished one successful lesson out of the day, then give yourself a mental 'pat on the back' that you have achieved this.

The challenge is now to learn how to sort out another lesson and another one until you have successfully negotiated the day. By focusing your efforts on the task, we would expect your self-confidence to rise, even if only a little. A start is better than spiralling further downwards.

 ### Activity 4.2

- In your journal, write down three accomplishments you made on your last time in school.
- What evidence can you suggest as to why you made these accomplishments?

  o For example, in your journal use the following statement and fill in the blanks:
  o 'I accomplished … This was demonstrated through/by … '

- As an example, you may have written:

  o 'I accomplished a practical lesson on shadows. This was demonstrated through all students completing the lesson objective of explaining to their partner what causes shadows, then making their own shadow puppet.'
  o 'I accomplished that the classroom was clean and tidy before the end of the lesson. This was demonstrated by the students having tidied away their books, all desks were clear, and that they were sitting ready for the bell.'

## Vicarious experience: learning from others

Vicarious experience is learning through watching others perform the task. If a teacher does not know the most effective way of teaching long multiplication, for example, he or she might benefit from watching an experienced teacher facilitate the lesson. Of course, this works in another way. If a teacher knows that they can effectively teach multiplication, this information confirms their capability and feeds back into their self-confidence.

## Verbal persuasion: providing encouragement

Confidence can be boosted through the use of encouraging statements and comments made by other people. In school, mentors and line managers usually occupy this role. However, in our experience, not enough positive feedback is handed out when things are going well. This may be because the sole focus of attention is usually only on achieving all outcomes successfully or teaching competencies. Anything less is perceived as failure. Not so! A good performance with a so-called 'poor' achievement of the learning outcomes or teaching competencies is not necessarily a failure if it means that the teacher has gained knowledge and experience for future use. By focusing on developing your technique, your confidence to succeed *will* also develop.

An important point to consider is the expertise and 'kudos' of the person who adopts this role or who is chosen by the teacher. If he or she has extensive experience, there is more likelihood that the teacher will believe and accept the comments being given. The simple message here is to use verbal persuasion to your advantage but do not fool yourself with comments that you know you don't believe.

Another type of verbal persuasion is self-talk, which is literally 'talking to yourself'. We discuss in detail how to use self-talk in Chapter 10. However, in terms of self-confidence, self-talk is an excellent way of building and retaining positive thoughts throughout the day. It will also help you to evaluate ongoing performance, so it provides a focus for your thoughts.

---

Self-confidence is boosted by constructive comment. When you are in the classroom there is nobody to provide verbal feedback (unless your students are particularly vocal!) so it becomes necessary for you to provide the feedback yourself.

---

By focusing on the process rather than the outcome, you will improve the way you negotiate each lesson and complete the day. You should then feed this information back into your teaching brain and praise yourself where it will give maximum impact.

 Activity 4.3

- Although we will go into more depth on self-talk in Chapter 10, for the moment, consider the following sentences:

  o 'I am in control of my classroom.'
  o 'I wish I could maintain everyone's attention.'

- o 'It would be great to have all resources ready at the start of the lesson.'
- o 'I can keep focused on the lesson objectives.'

- Which of these sentences appear to be the most beneficial in terms of building and retaining positive thoughts?
- The first and fourth are direct statements, whereas the second and third are aspirations which would have less impact.
- In your journal, note down one sentence which appeals to you ... or have a go at writing one that is personally meaningful.

## Physiological arousal

Physiological arousal is not as much a predictor of self-confidence as the other three elements outlined above and a discussion here will not provide many benefits to the teacher. Chapter 5, however, provides a more useful focus of attention for understanding how arousal influences the way in which we think. Suffice to say, it is how you interpret the signs from your body that influences your expectations about your performance. For example, if you are sitting in your classroom, ready for the morning bell and notice that you have sweaty palms and your heart rate has gone up, you may interpret these signs, as indicators of anxiety and your self-confidence will start to fade away. Yet, if you interpret the same signs as indicators of excitement and readiness, your self-confidence will remain high.

### Summary Box

Each of Bandura's elements influences our expectations about our performances, helping to provide feedback about our capability and aid self-confidence. If capability and self-confidence are high then the expectation to teach successfully also increases. As such, this relates to what was discussed about self-determination in the previous chapter.

## Symptoms associated with reduced self-confidence, and overcoming them

In working with a teacher, one of our early questions is, 'Tell me about a lesson where everything seemed to go wrong,' in order to tease out which aspect of self-confidence he or she feels is a problem. We can use this as an exercise in showing that perhaps not all aspects of the teacher's self-confidence are as damaged as he or she might think, especially when we follow with, 'Tell me about a lesson where everything seemed to go well.'

 **Activity 4.4**

- Before you read the next section, consider a lesson where everything went well. Briefly outline this lesson in your journal.
- Consider how you felt about this lesson. Make a note of these feelings.

It is vital to be aware of the symptoms associated with diminishing self-confidence. Without such knowledge, it is not possible to put strategies and procedures in place to change things. However, identifying symptoms is not an exact science and everybody is different. Nevertheless, we have compiled a list of possible symptoms below that may provide clues to present or emerging self-confidence issues.

## Negative emotions

Teachers lacking self-confidence may show signs of negative emotions. If this happens, *look for signs of tension and anxiety*, which may also be present. They may seem miserable all of the time or, for no apparent reason. Positive emotion is associated with a relaxed state of body and mind and allows teachers to assert themselves at critical moments in a lesson or a staff meeting where the outcome could go 'either way'.

## Reduced concentration

Teachers lacking self-confidence may show signs of not concentrating or focusing on the task at hand. Other issues are clouding their judgement and worry has taken a predominant role. Obviously, it is not possible to 'see' thought processes. Nevertheless, the signs are there. *If the teacher needs to frequently remind themself of important information, or seems distracted by the plethora of activity going on, he or she may be lacking concentration, which in turn may be influenced by a lack of self-confidence.* This highlights the interaction between many of the topics discussed in this book and how it is crucial to be able to identify signs and symptoms in order to implement effective interventions.

## Reduced effort

The effort a teacher puts into his or her preparation for the lesson is also linked to confidence. *If confidence is at an optimal level, effort tends to increase.* We have spoken to teachers who have 'given up' midway through a lesson because they have felt the lesson was going out of control. Even in a lesson where not every student will achieve the learning outcomes, we would still expect the teacher to put the effort in to push themselves. If the teacher seems not to be 'too fussed' about putting effort in, they may … and we stress only 'may', have self-confidence issues to resolve. Of course, there could be any number of other reasons and these would need to be explored systematically.

## Inappropriate goals

People who are lacking in self-confidence have a tendency to set goals that are easy to achieve, or set no goals at all. In either of these instances, there is no way that they can fail. If their goal was within easy reach, how can they expect to push themselves and increase in competence?

 **Reflection**

> Ask yourself objectively whether your goals are realistic, yet challenging. If they are not, you need to consider expanding them to give yourself room to succeed. Refer to Chapter 8 on goal setting for further information.

*If the goals set are questionable, then the teacher may be disguising lack of self-confidence with 'easily achievable' outcomes.*

## Inappropriate teaching strategies

In the classroom, teachers tend to adopt one of two types of strategy: succeeding with their teaching or focusing on not making mistakes. If a teacher lacks self-confidence, he or she will be more inclined to adopt the latter of these strategies, focusing on not making mistakes. They will adopt a teaching style and not teach the way that they would if confidence was high. A concern will be about making mistakes and, as we hope you would expect us to say, thinking about making mistakes places emphasis on making them and that is precisely what *will* happen. *Ask yourself whether you are teaching to succeed or focusing on not making mistakes.* If you are focusing on not making mistakes, you will then need to ask yourself why you are thinking in this way. You may need to change your teaching strategies. The chapters on goal setting (Chapter 8) and self-talk (Chapter 10) provide comprehensive guidance on this.

## Interrupted 'momentum'

At one point in the lesson, everything is running smoothly and according to plan. Suddenly, in the next moment everything seems to have fallen apart, that is, the momentum has gone. *A self-confident teacher will overcome this, with a never-say-die attitude and will bounce back during the lesson.* A teacher who lacks self-confidence will find this an extremely difficult, if not impossible, task. We would ask a teacher to identify whether they have ever experienced this situation and would perhaps suggest that goal setting would be an ideal way to keep their mind focused on the challenge rather than their apparent misperception of the situation. If your 'momentum' is interrupted, you will be less likely to enter 'the zone', where everything seems so easy.

## Summary of assessing and improving self-confidence

 **Activity 4.5**

By answering in your journal the questions below, you will gain an insight into your own perceived self-confidence. It is important that you provide yourself with honest answers, so that you can move forward and develop further.

When am I overconfident?
When do I experience self-doubt?
Is my confidence consistent during each lesson?
How do I recover from errors?
Am I indecisive or defensive in certain teaching situations?
How do I respond to adversity?
Do I relish the prospect of and enjoy teaching demanding lessons?

Improving self-confidence is not as difficult as it may at first appear. The key is to consider what psychologists call 'process', leaving 'outcome' as a side effect.

| | |
|---|---|
| Process | Focusing on *how* to do something |
| Outcome | Focusing on the end result |

In working with a teacher, one of the first things we may do would be to work through a mental imagery programme (see Chapter 11). By doing this, the teacher can learn to visualize him or herself performing successfully in the classroom. With practice, this visualization simulates what happens in the lesson, potentially strengthening connections in the brain so that split-second reactions and decisions are easier to make when teaching for real. The old adage of 'practice makes perfect' should be used when you are honing your mental skills. So, if you visualize negotiating the lesson successfully over and over again, your visualized performance will get stronger and stronger. When you do the same thing in reality, your performances will increase your self-confidence.

If mental imagery and goal setting are combined, there is no reason why a teacher's thought processes will not improve. If he or she begins to think positively and confidently, then they will begin to act confidently. Let us provide a day-to-day example. We would like you to start smiling and begin to laugh. Laugh a little louder. How do you feel? We would expect you to be feeling rather happier and more positive, than you were a moment ago. The same principle applies to self-confidence. If you act confidently, you are more likely to feel confident, as long as you also have the capability for the task in hand. **Change the way you think and you will change the way you act.** The key, as we have said elsewhere in this chapter, is to be realistic about your ability. You should also set achievable, yet challenging goals for yourself.

Physical fitness is another key to improving self-confidence. If you have the stamina and mental endurance to match your physical capabilities, there is no reason why self-confidence should not be high. If you acknowledge that your physical fitness is lacking, then embark on a training programme or seek help from a fitness instructor to improve this area of potential weakness. We are not suggesting that you need to embark on an exhaustive, time-consuming programme of pain-related athleticism. We are suggesting, however, that a good level of physical activity (of your choice) *will* help you.

## Ritual or routine?

*Implementing what psychologists call pre-performance routines is another way of improving self-confidence.* Some people talk more in terms of 'ritual'. As an example, prior to a demanding day of teaching, some people may always drive the same way to work, even though it may take longer. We have known teachers to wear their favourite tie clip, or carry their favourite pen. We have even come across a teacher who has five pairs of socks they wear solely for teaching (although not all at the same time!). Some people might argue that this is a ritual. We would prefer to talk in terms of things that teachers do as a routine before a day in the classroom ... everything has been considered and is ready. Forget about 'lucky socks'. It is more important that you feel comfortable in your appearance! ***Routines provide teachers with ultimate control***. For example, if a teacher establishes a structured plan or strategy for the week, then he or she will know what to do, when and for how long before critical moments loom on the horizon. It is important to establish routines, to provide a sense of security and familiarity. Without a structured regime, uncertainty may creep into the mind and wreak havoc on self-confidence.

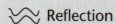 Reflection

Consider any routines you have developed prior to the start of a school day. There is no need to write this down – this is your routine: it is what works for you.

Self-confidence is inextricably linked with motivation and it is to this aspect of psychological functioning that we will turn in the next chapter.

## One-minute summary

This chapter has introduced the concept of self-confidence: *confidence* in having the belief that you can achieve and succeed; *self* in that it comes from you – you are in control. Self-confidence affects the way you perform in the classroom. Furthermore, self-confidence is situation specific, that is, you may feel confident in one situation and not in another.

You are in control of your self-confidence through looking for the positives in a situation and being aware of how to rectify areas you may not feel as confident with. Indeed, there are several strategies you can adopt to develop your self-confidence:

- Assess your performance – acknowledge what you do well.
- Learn from others – watch and listen to other experienced teachers.
- Gain encouragement from others – especially people whose opinion you value.
- Be aware of physiological symptoms – for example, physical indicators of diminished self-confidence.

There are a number of symptoms that indicate low self-confidence. Signs to look out for are:

- negative emotions, for example tension and anxiety;
- reduced concentration;
- reduced effort;
- inappropriate goals;
- inappropriate teaching strategies;
- interrupted momentum.

In order to develop your self-confidence further:

- Focus on how to do something (the process) as opposed to the end result (the outcome).
- Mentally rehearse aspects of the school day so that you are prepared for all eventualities.

## Short-term strategies for the here and now

- Consider areas of your teaching you are confident with. What are the success indicators for this?
- Focus on what you managed to achieve the last time you were in school – what went well?
- Consider one area you would like to become more confident with. Focus on how to achieve this by noting down a series of steps.
- Continue to verbalize mentally a positive sentence, for example, 'I am in control of my classroom'.

Mentally rehearse some aspect of the school day that you feel less confident with. Keep replaying this in your mind until it becomes second nature.

## Mentoring issues

Your mentor should be fundamental in helping your confidence through noting the successes you have achieved. They will be able to provide feedback on your progress, areas to consider developing and how these may be achieved. Your mentor should be able to help with your goal setting as well as advice on reaching these goals.

## Further reading

There are few books specifically discussing self-confidence and teaching; however, there are many books available on developing confidence. We have recommended a few here should you wish to develop further confidence-building strategies:

Burton, K. (2005) *Building Self-Confidence for Dummies*. Chichester: John Wiley & Sons.
Another recommended book from the '… for Dummies' series. This book is easy to 'dip into' with each chapter containing useful lists, activities, summaries, and so on, covering a range of related issues on self-confidence.

Litvinoff, S. (2007) *The Confidence Plan*. Harlow: BBC Active.
This book provides a 10-step plan to facilitate the reader in understanding where they are now and where they need to be, and how to achieve this. The book is easy to read, uses clear case studies and provides practical advice and exercises.

Preston, D.L. (2007) *365 Steps to Self-Confidence: A Complete Programme for Personal Transformation – In Just a Few Minutes a Day*. 3rd rev. edn. Oxford: How To Books.
This book contains 365 nuggets of information divided into 52 sections which discuss confidence across all aspects of life. It is in essence a workbook with practical activities to conduct, adhering to the author's 'Intention – Thinking – Imagination – Act' formula.

# 5

# I Can't Cope! Emotion, Mood and Stress

## Introduction

Performance in the classroom, as within all aspects of daily life, is influenced by emotional states, moods and responses to stressful events. In this chapter, we will discuss the effects of emotion, mood states and stress on your teaching. The good news is that these bodily states can be identified and changed so that they are no longer cause for concern. We will explore 'ways of thinking' about these states so that they do not interfere with your teaching. With practice, such states can be used to actually enhance your teaching performance. In the chapter on self-talk and cognitive restructuring, we outline how negative thoughts can adversely influence performance. We also show how these thoughts can be substituted with positive thoughts. The same technique can be used to identify emotional and mood states. It simply involves identifying the symptoms that seem to be causing a drop in performance and then dealing with them through cognitions, the way you think about those symptoms.

## Chapter objectives

- Consider the impact of emotions on teaching performance.
- Understand the causes of stress through the relationship between arousal and anxiety.
- Identify causes of anxiety through completing psychometric measures.
- Develop strategies for dealing with anxiety.

## Stress in the teaching profession

Stress and stress-related illness are significant within the teaching profession. According to the Health and Safety Executive, stress is a major cause of absence from work. In 2008 the National Association of Schoolmasters and Union of Women Teachers (NASUWT) reported that half a million working days are lost each year in the UK with teachers signed off with stress. Furthermore they note that 69 per cent of teachers have reported stress. Thankfully stress is becoming accepted as a major cause of absence and the stigma of 'not being able to cope' is lessening. The Japanese, however, have a term for stress which dates back to 1969 – *Karoshi* – or 'death from overwork'. Let's hope that the term doesn't catch on over here! Yet the important point is that teaching can be stressful and that as a unified profession, dealing with stress should be a priority.

## How do emotions and mood affect teaching performance?

Everyone experiences emotions during daily life. Indeed emotion and cognition, or thought processing, are inextricably linked. It is not possible to have one without the other. As the school day begins, you may feel happy and excited or nervous and uptight.

How you feel about the moment will always influence the reality of that moment. If you feel preoccupied, your focus will be taken away from the job in hand. If you are feeling positive about the day, it will, more often than not, work in your favour and you will seamlessly flow into the first lesson as the students arrive. So, emotion can be thought of as experiencing feelings of joy, fear, anger, interest as well as threat, sadness and disgust. *Emotions are also multifaceted, in that they can be subjective, biological, social, or purposeful in nature*. The subjective experience of emotion is 'how does the emotion make me feel?' Biologically, the same question applies, but this is linked to how you feel physiologically rather than psychologically. For example, how you interpret the sudden increase in heart rate you have just experienced considers emotion from a physiological or biological viewpoint. Socially, emotion is the visual signal of the emotional state you wish to display to the world. A teacher may portray body language suggesting contentment, happiness and interest in the class, but they may be feeling nervous by a forthcoming observation. Emotion is linked directly to motivation and was covered in Chapter 3.

 Reflection

Note down examples of where you have displayed one emotion to others but have physically felt a different emotion. For example, perhaps you have been angry with another motorist but have kept a calm demeanour. Can you provide examples that are school specific?

You might be forgiven for thinking that the term, 'emotion' has almost negative connotations. It suggests that rational thought is being displaced by irrational thought. But if emotion and cognition are inextricably linked, then it is important to harness emotions and use them in your favour rather than against you. This is where identifying how you feel at various points in time becomes important. If emotions are influenced by everyday life events and how we interpret those events, moods colour those emotions. *The way in which you feel about an event will be coloured by the mood that you find yourself in at this moment*. Moods can change rapidly and, indeed, it is not always possible to explain a sudden shift in mood.

Where emotions are varied, moods fall into one of two categories: positive or negative, that is, good moods or bad moods. Performing while in a positive mood invariably provides an enjoyable time in the classroom. In contrast, a negative mood is reflected in irritability, dissatisfaction and ultimately in a 'bad day at the office'.

 Activity 5.1

- Divide a page in half. On one side put the title 'Positive Moods', on the other, 'Negative Moods'.
- Spend five minutes listing as many emotions as you can under each heading.

*(Continued)*

*(Continued)*

- Are there any emotions which are context dependent ... that could be placed under both positive and negative moods?
- Being aware of how different emotions can influence your mood is a first step in trying to develop the positive moods while limiting the negative. To this extent, consider a couple of the positive emotions. Note down what you could do to bring about this emotion.

***Positive moods are also thought to influence the brain's biochemistry.*** Part of the brain contains a system of nerves that act as a 'reward pathway'. In short, this means that the brain seeks the next 'hit', akin to addiction. Let us start here with an evolutionary example. The act of intercourse at the point of orgasm provides an intense physiological pleasure that 'rewards' the brain for its activities. Having experienced it for the first time, we set out to seek it time and time again. We crave the reward previously experienced thus ensuring the survival of the species. Any experience that provides a great deal of pleasure can act in the same way. Arguably, teaching provides a similar element of intense physiological pleasure; we teach because of the addictive 'hit' it provides. So, ***mood affects performance both psychologically and physiologically***. It is how you interpret, or misinterpret these physiological signals that can influence your teaching positively or negatively. Although it is quite acceptable to go in search of this physiological reward, it is important to bear in mind that teachers need to remain objective about the information they are assessing. If you lose sight of the 'wider picture' it is easy to misinterpret information. The 'applied' chapters in Section 3, together with this chapter will help to highlight the signals and symptoms to look out for.

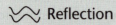 Reflection

Consider what you find 'rewarding' from teaching. Compare this to the Reflection in Chapter 3 on intrinsic motivation. Are there any differences?

So, physiology plays an important role in the way information is interpreted by the teaching brain. You will be familiar with stress from your own experiences. There will have been days when everything seemed to go wrong. An unexpected disturbance, resource failure (photocopier, ICT, and so on), illness ... the list goes on. How you dealt with those

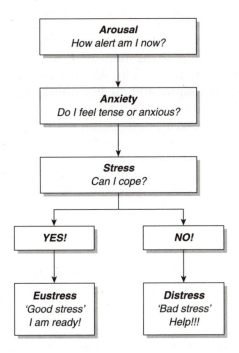

**Diagram 5.1** Relationship between arousal, anxiety and stress (adapted from Jones, 1995)

problems psychologically dictated how you performed during the day. Were you overly nervous in the classroom? Did you lack the feel and finesse usually present in your teaching? Were you preoccupied with trivial occurrences that 'played on your mind'? Did you feel under more pressure than normal? Any of these things could have been present because you were unable to cope with the situation, or because you interpreted your own feelings of physiological arousal incorrectly. If you did, then you put yourself into a position of stress.

In order to define the term stress, it is necessary to put things into perspective by going back two steps, to bring in the concepts of arousal and anxiety. As such, stress is the overall process of interpreting the body's state of arousal in an anxious or non-anxious manner (Diagram 5.1).

We shall consider each of these elements in turn, in order to build up a picture of how the situation escalates to a point where stress becomes too much and performance drops as a consequence.

## Arousal

Arousal can be thought of as both a physiological and psychological state. As you read this chapter, inevitably you are experiencing a state of physiological arousal. Your heart rate is perhaps nestling around 70 beats per minute, your pupils are no more dilated than normal, your breathing is slow, relaxed and your body is in a state of balance or equilibrium. Psychologically, you are perhaps motivated to read on, processing the information on this page successfully. Alternatively, you might have just finished the previous chapter and are beginning to lose concentration. Your mind is perhaps in need of a break before you return.

If we consider a teacher's physiological arousal before a lesson, the story differs completely. *As the lesson beckons, we would expect your state of physiological arousal to change*. We would like to think that your arousal increases to an optimal level, so you are physiologically ready to perform at an optimal level when the lesson begins.

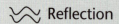 Reflection

Consider an undulating graph of arousal as the day progresses. Are there certain 'peaks' when your arousal is at the optimum level?

Again, it is possible to explain this state in evolutionary terms. The human body possesses a defence mechanism in response to danger. Deep in our ancestry this has helped to prevent us from being eaten by predators. It is a so-called 'fight-or-flight' response. Of course, there is little chance of being eaten by predators so one might think that the response is no longer necessary. This is not the case. Indeed, the fight-or-flight response still protects us today from modern-day equivalents of predators. If you trip as you are walking down a set of stairs, your heart rate will increase immediately, providing oxygenated blood to the muscles, your pupils will dilate and you will automatically put a hand out to grab the rail. You are responding to the danger to protect yourself from harm. There is no element of cognition involved. It merely happens: the fight-or-flight response kicks in automatically to prepare you for the danger, which, by this time is too late and has already happened.

Hans Selye developed a conceptual model to explain a person's physiological response to stressful situations of this type (Selye, 1956). The model comprises three stages: alarm reaction, resistance and exhaustion. The alarm reaction is another term for fight-or-flight, as explained above. This is the immediate, short-term response to a stressful, 'emergency' situation. If the stressful situation occurs over a longer period, the human body goes into endurance mode and begins to resist or cope with the demands. In terms of teaching, this would be similar to the teacher who performs well in the first half of a teaching experience, or half term, and is under pressure to retain this level for the remainder

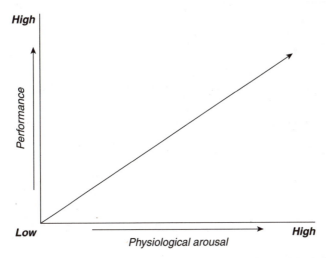

**Diagram 5.2**   The 'drive theory': performance–arousal relationship (adapted from Hull, 1943)

of the experience/term. This pressure however is likely to be self-induced. If they fail to maintain their standard in the classroom, it may be that coping with the situation has depleted the body's resources and the teacher is now exhausted in the physiological sense of the word. *The human body will invariably become depleted of its fuels in the same way that the engine will deplete its supply of petrol*. Both need refu-elling at appropriate moments. We will discuss this in more detail later in this chapter, when we go on to talk about stress from a psychological perspective.

Early psychologists saw the relationship between arousal and per-formance as linear, that is *the higher the arousal, the better the performance*. This sounds appealing and seems to confirm the idea of getting 'psyched up' for the teacher. This 'drive theory' can be seen in Diagram 5.2.

It seems therefore, that a simple solution to the arousal issue would be to find out what that optimal level of arousal is, so that you can reach that heightened state. Not quite! It may be the case that your arousal level has built up so much over the course of the term that it is too high and may in fact be detrimental to your per-formance. In this instance, you would need to reduce your arousal to optimal levels. This leads us nicely on to what theorists call the 'inverted-U hypothesis' also known as the Yerkes-Dodson Law (Yerkes and Dodson, 1908). Put simply and as illustrated in Diagram 5.3, *performance improves as arousal levels increase to an optimal level*. If this optimal level is exceeded, performance begins to take a drop and suffers.

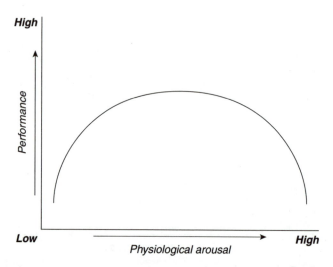

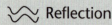

**Diagram 5.3**   The 'inverted-U theory': performance–arousal relationship (adapted from Yerkes and Dodson, 1908)

〰 Reflection

> Consider what would happen if your arousal levels got to a 'critical point'. How would you know this? What could you do about it?

Neither theory fully explains what is happening when situations suddenly deteriorate. This is where the so-called 'Catastrophe Theory' offers us some idea of what may be happening in our heads. Fazey and Hardy (1988) suggest that increased physiological arousal is right as long as cognitive anxiety remains low. So this means that if your thought processes start spiralling out of control, you are more likely experience a 'catastrophic' event; you will do something wrong and perhaps very silly! On the other hand, if your physiological arousal is high but you are in control of your thought processes, then it will be 'business as usual'.

〰 Reflection

> - Consider an event in the past where both your arousal was high as was your cognitive anxiety. Note down the event, including what led to it (the antecedent) and what happened (the consequence).
> - With hindsight (a very valuable thing!) how could the event have been handled differently? Indeed, this places you into a mentoring capacity, someone whose hindsight can become your foresight. Indeed, hindsight explains the injury that foresight would have prevented!

A basic measure of physiological arousal can be obtained using heart rate monitors, such as those developed by Polar. Alternatively, be aware of the physiological symptoms of increased heart rate (for example, shortness of breath, clammy hands, tense muscles and 'butterflies' in the stomach).

If you are aware that your heart rate is too high, or indeed too low, you must ask the question, 'Why?' What events led to that situation, what was your perception of those events and was that perception appropriate for the circumstances? It is at this point that we need to return to the inverted-U hypothesis. Although it appears to offer us answers to the arousal–performance relationship, it does not address these vital psychological factors that play a role in how we perform. In order to take this line of discussion further we shall introduce the concept of anxiety and go on to discuss two of its sub-types: somatic anxiety and cognitive anxiety.

## Anxiety

We would anticipate that every person who picks up the book to read this chapter will have experienced anxiety in some form or another. We all feel 'anxious' at times during our daily lives. This anxiety may, and usually does, manifest itself when we compete. But do we really know what anxiety is? Do we know how to identify which type of anxiety we may be suffering from, or whether we are in serious trouble, suffering from both types? Do we know how to control our anxiety when necessary? We suspect not. This section addresses these questions. We will begin by exploring the idea that individuals may be predisposed to anxiety (a character 'trait'), while it may also manifest itself with the forthcoming situation (a specific 'state'). We will then deal with somatic and cognitive anxiety.

Trait anxiety is a predisposition towards anxiety. Perhaps you are an anxious person in many situations. If this were the case, you might say that this is one of your many traits, or characteristics that make up who you are. In terms of teaching, it could mean that you would experience a high level of anxiety towards the lesson, because it is in your nature. In contrast, state anxiety is a reaction towards a specific event. You are not usually anxious about any particular lesson, but today in this lesson, you are suddenly feeling really anxious.

Although both these types of anxiety would appear, and indeed can be, damaging, the role of a psychologist is to help teachers identify whether they are trait-anxious individuals or whether they suffer from state anxiety. It then becomes possible to put interventions in place to overcome any difficulties that these may be causing. Among other things we would discuss with a teacher is how they feel about their 'nerves'. If trait anxiety is established to be an area of concern, the psychologist and teacher will work through the underlying sources of the anxiety, changing the way in which these sources are thought about.

**Table 5.1**   Questions to ask prior to your teaching 'performance'

 1  Am I feeling nervous before I teach?
 2  Am I experiencing self-doubt with my teaching abilities?
 3  Does my stomach feel 'knotted' prior to teaching?
 4  Am I concerned about not coping under the pressure of teaching?
 5  Am I feeling 'jittery' prior to teaching?
 6  Am I concerned that I might not do as well I could do?
 7  Am I concerned about a previous 'failure' within my teaching?
    *If your answer to the questions above is 'yes', Chapters 9–12 will help you to reduce teaching state anxiety.*
 8  Is my body feeling tense prior to teaching?
 9  Am I feeling ready to teach?
10  Does my body feel relaxed?
11  Am I feeling 'comfortable'?
12  Am I feeling self-confident about my teaching abilities?
13  Am I feeling at ease?
14  Do I feel that I can meet the challenge of teaching?
    *If your answer to questions 8–14 is 'yes', you appear not to have any teaching anxiety. Well done! If it is 'no', Chapters 9–12 will help you to reduce your anxiety.*

*Source*: Derived from Martens et al., 1990

Chapter 10 on self-talk and cognitive restructuring is useful in helping to remedy the situation. Do not think for a moment that if you are identified as being a highly trait-anxious person, that the situation is irredeemable! As with trait anxiety, state anxiety can be measured by questionnaires, used in conjunction with interview and discussion.

A common state anxiety questionnaire in use at present is the Competitive State Anxiety Inventory–2, which measures both somatic (or physiological) anxiety and cognitive (or mental) anxiety, as well as confidence, and looks at the present, the here-and-now of the performance, rather than the generalized view of anxiety that exists with the trait approach.

The sample questions in Table 5.1 are derived from the Competitive State Anxiety Inventory–2 (Martens et al., 1990). They are used for illustrative purposes to provide you with an idea of the kind of questions you should ask yourself before you teach. Although this questionnaire is used with performing competitors, we see teaching as a performance, therefore the questionnaire is valid. Let's face it, if you're not competing with anyone else, you are competing with yourself to become a better teacher.

## Additional self-test questions (trait anxiety)

The questions in Table 5.2 relate to your general performance in all aspects of your life. As previously noted, 'trait' relates to your underlying, day-to-day, attributes.

**Table 5.2**   Questions about your trait anxiety

1   Do I often feel uneasy?
2   Do I often worry about making mistakes?
3   Do I often worry about not performing well?
4   Do I often feel 'queasy'?
    *If your answer to the questions above is 'yes', Chapter 11 will help you to change the way you think about your trait-anxiety.*
5   Do I find competing against others socially enjoyable?
6   Am I generally a calm person?
7   Is setting goals important to me?
8   Do I enjoy competing in activities that require considerable amounts of physical energy?
9   Do I often notice my heart 'racing'?
    *If your answer to questions 5–8 is 'yes', you appear not to experience trait anxiety. If it is 'no', Chapter 11 will help you to change the way you think about your trait anxiety and this may change with a little work from you. Question 9 is dependent on how you view an increase in heart rate. If you view it as a way of providing you with a rich supply of oxygenated blood to the brain, this is a good thing. If you view it as 'unnerving', it is contributing to your anxiety and needs to be changed.*

If we accept that you are not high in trait anxiety, we would then direct attention to the specific event. In order to explore pre-teaching state anxiety we need to examine somatic and cognitive anxiety in greater depth. As previously noted, the word 'somatic' means 'of the body'. *Symptoms of somatic anxiety are therefore physical and related to the body.* Table 5.3 lists some of the more common elements, or symptoms of somatic anxiety. Look through the list and tick those that you have experienced before a lesson.

If you experience these types of symptoms before teaching, the next question we would have is, 'At what point do you experience them … minutes before the lesson, an hour before, a day before, etc.?' In establishing when the symptoms emerge, it becomes possible for the psychologist to introduce relaxation techniques to help eradicate these symptoms. It also allows him or her to explore the reasons underlying

**Table 5.3**   Questions relating to somatic anxiety

| Symptom | Tick if applicable |
| --- | --- |
| Increased perspiration | |
| Clammy, sweaty hands | |
| Dryness in the mouth | |
| Increased need to urinate | |
| 'Butterflies' in the stomach | |
| Increased heart rate | |
| Nausea | |
| Muscle tension | |
| Physical tiredness | |
| Irritability | |

their emergence. It is convenient now to explore cognitive anxiety, which may be responsible for producing some of these physical symptoms.

*Cognitive anxiety is basically 'worry'*. It is that portion of anxiety that is influenced by thought processes. Thought processes are used to appraise various situations that you may find yourself in. A negative appraisal of these situations is the precursor to cognitive anxiety and may, in extreme situations, lead to the phenomenon known as *'choking' or 'freezing'*. This can be inferred in situations such as bringing the students to attention to proceed with a lesson. You know you need a good start to capture attention, to hook the students into the lesson, yet as you are about to speak, your mouth is dry and you stumble over your words, unable to make that smooth start you had envisaged. (One of the reasons why we always write down our first sentence before we teach!) In addition, worry about future events or situations and their outcomes or consequences is an element of cognitive anxiety (Lavallee et al., 2004). This implies that fear of failure and worry about what people might think about your performance are important determinants of anxiety. *We would strive to help teachers restructure the way in which they appraise important situations*. This is covered in more detail in Chapter 10.

The message is, however, very clear. Anxiety can be debilitating. *It can get in the way of routines, strategy, rational thought processes and can upset the psychological balance necessary for calm, controlled performance*. This is what we mean when we say that we are experiencing stress. As illustrated earlier in this chapter, it is a state of what Selye (1983) called 'distress'. Ironically, anxiety can also be facilitating. In contrast, Selye coined the term 'eustress' for the facilitating effects of anxiety. It is shorthand for 'euphoric stress', where the body is in a positive state because of the way the 'stress' is being interpreted. As such then, the word 'stress' becomes redundant in the term 'euphoric stress'. For the purpose of clarity, we would prefer to use the term, 'euphoric readiness', thus removing any connotations to the negative terminology present in the word, 'stress'. When we call this a facilitative state, we mean that the positive 'spin' placed on how you are thinking about your teaching is working for you rather than against you. You are happy that the thought processes are working as efficiently as they can. *Your perception of the challenge is, therefore, vital in controlling the level of cognitive anxiety that you experience*. If you lose it in your head, your body will tense up, this information will feed back into your head and you will interpret it in a negative way. A vicious spiral then emerges and a so-called *'catastrophe'* will happen. Indeed, as we mentioned earlier in this chapter, the term 'catastrophe' has been used by psychologists to explain sudden drops in performance that seem to arise from nowhere.

Fazey and Hardy argue that if cognitive anxiety is relatively high and arousal levels are low, performance will be optimal. If, however, cognitive

**Table 5.4**   Stages to reduce anxiety

| | |
|---|---|
| Step 1 | Identify the demand placed upon you |
| Step 2 | Identify your perception of that demand |
| Step 3 | Ascertain your psychological and physiological response to that perception |
| Step 4 | Substitute inappropriate thoughts where necessary |
| Step 5 | Observe/reflect/record your behaviour in response to the situation |

anxiety is relatively high and arousal levels are also high, performance will suffer considerably. *For teaching, the key is to identify a level of arousal at which you feel comfortable to perform.* You should then focus on the kind of thoughts that run through your mind before and during the lesson and identify whether they are acceptable or not (whether they are positive or negative). If there are any negative thoughts, substitute them through cognitive restructuring. Finally, *combine the positive thought processes with your preferred level of arousal and you have a recipe for success!* Table 5.4 summarizes this for you.

Of course, it is all very easy for us to sit here and provide a recipe for success, but when things are not going well, it is easy to lose sight of the way towards a solution. In this next section, we will cover the negative aspects of stress in more detail, before going on to explain ways of identifying and coping with it.

 Activity 5.2

Review Table 5.4. Identify one of your current demands and work through the five steps.

## Where do your stresses come from?

Stress comes from either personal or situational sources. Although there are measures that assess how much stress a person is facing within their work, for example, it is the interplay between both personal and professional stressors that lead to stress. If you have to work long hours to complete your work, this will affect, for example, your quality of sleep or quality of relationships, and vice versa. We will look at the professional and personal perspective of change in the next chapter.

The importance of an event and the role of uncertainty within that event are common sources of stress among teachers; for example, some teachers' stress levels rise significantly when the inspectors are in. Focusing on the importance of the 'event' undermines the day-to-day teaching that teachers effectively engage with. *Event importance is a key factor in raising stress levels.* Yet event importance is only a label. If you do not allow yourself to be 'sucked in' to the hype and, instead, **treat the event as any other, then you will minimize its importance, thus enabling you to concentrate on the process of teaching** when your colleagues are focusing on the 'what if I fail to perform' scenario.

The uncertainty of a situation may undoubtedly have an adverse effect on your teaching, but only if you are not in control of environmental factors. **The key therefore, is to establish the greatest degree of control you can.** This might mean discussing appropriate issues with anyone (the headteacher, the mentor, and so on) to ensure that everything that can possibility be done in support of your focus is being done.

 Activity 5.3

Make a note of all the events or situations that have been causing you stress recently. You could start through exploring the 'Schedule of Recent Experience' which is widely available on the Internet. This is a list of 42 questions although some of these are probably not relevant.

From your list of stressors, try and categorize them. How you do this is dependent on each person. Typical categories could be:

Work
Home
Financial
Family
Relationships
Health
Social activities

From categorizing the stressors, apply a rating:

1 – I can take control of this
2 – I should be able to control this
3 – I lack control over this
4 – HELP!

Total your responses for each category to determine the category providing the greatest source of stress. From here the strategy for negating these stressors may start to become evident. An example would be continual pain may cause disturbed sleep, which in turn means you are unable to concentrate fully on your work, which means you have to work longer hours, which means your relationships suffer ... we're sure you get the picture.

From this, a visit to the GP to discuss the impact of your health on your work may result in visiting an occupational therapist who can help facilitate strategies for coping with your health.

We discussed self-esteem in relation to confidence in Chapter 4, but the lower one's self-esteem, which is based on the perception of one's ability, the higher anxiety is likely to be. The consequence is a potential dip in performance, or, the failure to reach one's potential in the first place.

It is widely accepted among psychologists that what is important here is the need to consider how personal factors interact with environmental factors to produce or to minimize stress. *Remember, stress is in your head. It is only real if you let it become real. By changing the way in which you think about these factors, you are exerting control over the situation.* Teachers should be well versed in Psychological Skills Training (PST) such as imagery, self-talk and goal setting, in order to cope with stress and anxiety. The PST chapters detailed in Section 3 provide the keys to unlocking your potential to control anxiety as you choose.

## One-minute summary

Stress is a significant aspect in the teaching profession that needs addressing. It should be seen as a priority within schools as a point of action for continual development, after all, schools are your employer and they have a duty of care to look after you.

Stress is an interplay of arousal and anxiety. Some stress is needed to motivate us, yet too much is demotivating. There is no one single cause of stress: different causes affect different people in different ways. It can arise from anywhere! One way of diagnosing stress is remembering that 'if you feel stressed, you are stressed'.

If you are experiencing stress, three simple avenues to explore are hydration, diet, fitness and sleep. Any imbalance between these factors may be contributing to stress. Fatigue, dehydration, lack of sleep and poor fitness may be affecting your concentration, focus, response and many other aspects of your teaching. These will be covered in the next chapter.

## Short-term strategies for the here and now

As with all of the short-term strategies, these are dealing with the consequence and not the cause. It is vital to ascertain what is causing the stress to be able to deal with it. Some suggested strategies are:

- *Visit your General Practitioner.* If you feel stressed, you are stressed! Stress can cause numerous effects on the body – remember prevention is better than a cure.
- *Go for a sports massage.* Don't feel you need to be a sportsperson to avail yourself of this resource. We often book a sports massage at the University of Worcester's Sport Therapy Department, when marking loads have been heavy. The beauty of this facility is that it provides students with the opportunities to practise on 'live bodies', while we get to reduce our tension levels, all at a nominal charge. No doubt

there are other places offering such services. Our advice would be to check with your local university or technical college, where volunteers are always needed, before embarking on more costly options.

- *Pressure points.* Use of pressure points, or finger-tip massage can provide some instant relief from stress. A couple of easy and safe techniques are outlined here, however visiting a qualified acupressure or reflexology practitioner is fundamental should you wish to explore this further.

  Two key points that are easy to find and safe to use are:

  o The point located above the bridge of the nose between the eyebrows. Gentle fingertip pressure applied in either a circular motion or pumping in and out of the point, for about two minutes will help.
  o The point located on the palm side of the hand, on the wrist crease, directly below the little finger. There is a bony protrusion and the point is next to that, in a small indentation. Press for thirty seconds with moderate to firm pressure, gradually releasing the pressure.

- *Review the various exercises in Chapters 9, 10 and 11.* The various exercises and 'Short-term strategies for the here and now' will provide useful information.

## Mentoring issues

It is imperative that you discuss with your mentor feelings of stress as soon as you feel they may be present. This is fundamental and your mentor will expect you to be open with them. Burying your feelings and not discussing them will only make things worse – yet your mentor may well be able to offer sound advice to help limit the stressor. If you don't want to admit you are stressed, it would be worth discussing how your mentor deals with the pressure of the job (avoiding the 's' word) and opening the discussion from there.

## Further reading

Carlson, R. (1997) *Don't Sweat the Small Stuff ... and It's All Small Stuff: Simple Ways to Keep the Little Things from Taking Over Your Life.* London: Hodder and Stoughton.
This book provides a series of strategies to regain your perspective.

Davis, M., Eshelman, E.R. and McKay, M. (2000) *The Relaxation and Stress Reduction Workbook.* 5th edn. Oakland, CA: New Harbinger Publications.
The workbook is an international bestseller and encompasses many different aspects to promote relaxation while decreasing stress. It is very detailed and has a series of practical exercises supported with theoretical perspectives.

Elkin, A. (1999) *Stress Management for Dummies*. Hoboken, NJ: Wiley.
Another of the 'for Dummies' books. Again, practical, informative and easy to work with.

Joseph, R. (2000) *Stress Free Teaching: A Practical Guide to Tackling Stress in Teaching, Lecturing and Tutoring*. London: Kogan Page.
This is one of the key books that discusses stress in relation to teaching, although tends to be focused more on the theoretical side of managing stress within the workplace than a series of strategies for immediate use.

Sapolsky, R.M. (2004) *Why Zebras Don't Get Ulcers*. New York: St. Martin's Press.
The premiss to this book is that humans are designed like zebras – to contend with potentially stressful situations immediately and in the short term (like being chased by a lion), opposed to the day-after-day long-term stress we experience in our modern society. This book is written in a humorous, witty style, with useful stories to demonstrate the key concepts.

# Flexibility for Action! Adapting to Change

## Introduction

'It is not the strongest species that survive, nor the most intelligent, but the ones who are most responsive to change.' (Although this is usually attributed to Charles Darwin, the actual origin remains debatable.)

Since it came into existence, the National Curriculum has been revised on six occasions, which averages a change every three years. We predict that yet another revision will be imminent! Similarly, it would appear that there is a new government initiative for implementation on a yearly, if not termly, basis. Alas, you need to ask whether you will add to the staffroom protests of 'Why can't they just leave education alone for once?' or whether you will embrace such change. Of course, the staffroom cynics would note, 'there are no new ideas in education' implying that if you stay in education long enough, trends will come into and go out of fashion in continual cycles.

Like it or not, the only certainty we have within education is the inevitability of change ... yet how can we prepare ourselves to adapt and embrace such changes? This chapter thus explores a range of issues relating to change, specifically highlighting where change comes from, how you may react to change and how to influence people to accept change. There are many different perspectives in relation to organizational management through to the psychology of change, and how this influences education. This chapter provides an overview of some of the process specifically focusing on how to work with change.

## Chapter objectives

- Understand the causes and nature of change.
- Identify how management is different to leadership.
- Recognize the impact of change on individuals.
- Appreciate how change affects individuals psychologically.
- Consider assertiveness strategies for coping with imposed changes.
- Develop strategies for working with change.

## Where does change come from?

Anywhere! Change can emerge from many different sources: in the introduction to this chapter, we used examples from the macro level (the wider perspective) for example, the government. Yet change may also come from the micro level (the narrower perspective), for example, within your local education authority, your school or even within your classroom. For this, consider timetable changes, through to new pupils on your register. Indeed if the world didn't change, things would become quite stagnant, boring and ... Darwin might turn in his grave!

One of the first aspects to consider, however, is where change comes from so that we can understand why the change is happening: if we can see the reason, we are more likely to engage with the development.

To this extent, change could be instigated through a number of areas:

- Social changes: consider the instigation and development of *Every Child Matters*.
- Economic changes: how has the 'global downturn' impacted on education?
- Knowledge/skills economy: what do we need to prepare our students for today so that they can take the lead from us tomorrow?
- Technological advancements: who remembers using a chalk board, overhead projector, BBC computers, or the smell of the spirit used for the Banda machine? No doubt we're showing our age … ask the 'more senior' teachers if you haven't a clue what we're going on about!
- Health, safety and environmental aspects: how have accidents (for example, on school trips) had an impact? Has your school implemented a carbon emissions policy?
- Food policy changes? Has your school implemented a healthy eating programme (as we discuss in the next chapter)?

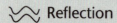

### Reflection

Consider a change you are currently engaged with. Where was the original source for this change?

Although change can arise from the micro to the macro, the impact can be small or large scale. As an example, one macro change of government initiative may impact more on the management of the school and have little impact currently on you. Alternately, on the micro level, your school may have appointed a new headteacher, who is making significant changes. Indeed, it may be that you are making changes to your practice or perhaps have been given the responsibility for leading a new development. To this extent, Diagram 6.1 identifies the varying levels of change.

If the suggested change is minor, this obviously has less impact and, as such, most people will regard this positively as a natural evolution. Yet it is the larger changes which have the greater impact. Schön (1983) highlights that such change initiatives often fail; although it may be easy to raise awareness for the required change, actually ensuring that staff are committed to the process is more difficult. As Schön notes, resistance to change is normal and should even be expected. This resistance occurs due to people feeling threatened in relation to their authority, power, territory and influence.

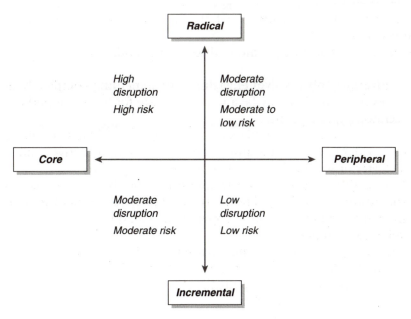

**Diagram 6.1** The quadrants of change (adapted from Blackwell, 2003)

- Threats to authority: in relation to authority, if you are trying to influence change as a new member of staff, you may be asking long-standing staff to question their professional practice. Such staff may have 'higher' positions within the school.
- Threats to power: associated with authority is 'power'. Will the proposed change enable others or disable others through taking away their influence?
- Threats to territory: perhaps the change is infringing on other people's areas of responsibility.
- Threats to influence: perhaps a member of staff had influence over a school policy when it was first developed, yet a new change may threaten their established work.

## The nature of change

Change is not just one singular aspect: it is anything which threatens a person's professional or personal existence, requiring them to re-evaluate their relationship with the previous norm. If the process of change can be understood in terms of why it needs to come about, then a person can start adapting psychologically (for guidance, see the chapter on goal setting). To this extent, the actual nature of change is one of the first aspects to consider ... what is actually going on? What is the proposed change?

Change can take one (or more) directions resulting in:

- Innovation: this involves engaging with something completely new. An example of this may be a new procedure for writing reports, new technology, and so on.
- Growth and expansion: this relates to doing more of the same, perhaps on a wider basis. As an example, consider how an initiative trialled in a cluster of schools may become the norm elsewhere.
- Contraction: this relates to the opposite of the above, in doing less of something (a rarity, we know!) For example, your school may have limited the amount of photocopying you can do, or the type of food 'allowed' in school.
- Diversification, or adapting existing practices to incorporate new elements. Consider how the curriculum has changed in one area or more. What has been 'amplified'?

 ## Activity 6.1

Consider how the following have impacted on you professionally:

- Innovation
- Growth and expansion
- Contraction
- Diversification

Reflecting on your responses, can you categorize the different areas of change from those with the most impact to those with the least?

What types of professional change do you feel will impact on your practice over the coming year?

## Managing the process of change

Although you may be relatively new to the teaching profession, it is likely that before long you will be responsible for implementing changes (if you are not already). Yet how can change be effectively facilitated? What steps do you need to take?

One model of change is 'Krüger's Iceberg' (Diagram 6.2). This model highlights a number of aspects for consideration. According to Krüger, most managers of change only tend to consider the tip of the iceberg – the management of the issues relating to cost, quality and time. Yet as

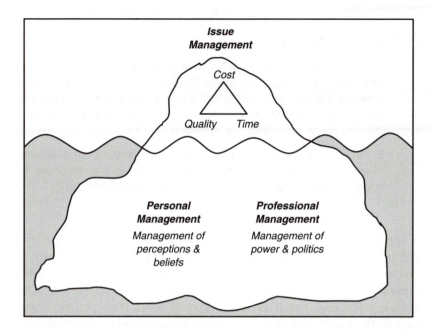

**Diagram 6.2** Krüger's Iceberg model of change (adapted from Krüger, 2002)

you are probably aware with icebergs, there are some nasty aspects that lurk under the surface of the water; these are the barriers to change. Specifically these are to do with managing the perceptions and beliefs of others, also managing power and politics within the school. Such barriers to change have one thing in common ... people!

## The personal perspective of power and politics

(Isn't alliteration a wonderful literary tool?) There are different types of people who you will encounter when trying to implement change; indeed, you may recognize yourself in one of the groups. According to Hritz (2008), out of a group where change is being introduced:

- 15 per cent embrace change;
- 60 per cent are uncertain of change;
- 25 per cent resist change.

A further consideration is whether individuals may overtly display all the positive signs for the change, yet have a 'hidden' negative attitude. By this, they may do all the right things asked of them, yet covertly they may try to undermine the change.

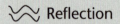 **Reflection**

Consider a recent staff meeting at your school where a change has been proposed. Out of a team of 10 staff, one or two members will embrace the change, two or three will actively resist change and the rest will be uncertain. What emotions, reactions and behaviours did you recognize within the meeting?

If you were the person responsible for implementing the proposed change, how could you encourage those who are uncertain to become active supporters? What strategies would you use?

As we have previously noted, change can be unsettling due to the threat to authority, power, territory and influence. Indeed, from this we have also highlighted that *change affects people professionally and personally*. The personal aspect is seldom considered as reflected in Krüger's Iceberg, yet it is this personal level that people have to engage with due to the 'upset' of their 'comfort zone' (something we will return to later in the chapter). Thus, in order to ensure change is introduced effectively, instigators of change need to ensure that the threats are lowered while recognizing that there is an element of personal discomfort, again which needs lowering. If headteachers, managers, or those with responsibility for change kept these two elements in mind, the impact on embedding such change would be significant in lowering stress levels (see Chapter 5). In relation to this, a subtle question could be asked: 'Is the person responsible for change, managing the change … or leading the change?'

## Management and leadership

What is the difference? What is preferable? Perhaps an analogy may help differentiate here. Consider David Brent from the television sitcom *The Office*, whose inept management 'style' is obvious in the extreme, and Mel Gibson's infamous and highly rousing battle speech in the film *Braveheart*. Both are in the elevated position of holding responsibility. Yet who would you classify as the leader and who as the manager? Hopefully this distinction may help you appreciate the differences.

Taking this further, Charles Handy (a key influence on professional change) provides a useful quote highlighting the differences:

Managing change is wishful thinking – it implies that one not only knows where to go and how to get there but persuades everyone else to travel there also.

> To cultivate change is different, suggesting an attitude of growth, channelling rather than controlling, of learning, not instruction. (Handy, 1993: 292)

Indeed, this notion of cultivating change is not new. Read through the following reflection.

## ⌇ Reflection

With the greatest headteacher above them,
staff barely know one exists.
Next comes one whom they love and praise.
Next comes one whom they fear.
Next comes one whom they despise and defy.

When a headteacher trusts no one,
No one trusts them.

The great headteacher speaks little.
They never speak carelessly.
They work without self-interest
and leave no trace.
When all is finished, the people say,
'We did it ourselves'.

To what extent is this relevant in your school? Is this the type of headteacher you may want to become one day?

Read through this quote again. Where do you think it comes from? When do you think it was written? (The answer is at the end of the chapter.)

The quote appears to effectively identify that those with the most influence, those who are respected and who can engage others, have leadership qualities. Indeed if you have looked at the answer, you will realize that the word 'headteacher' has replaced 'leader'. In highlighting the differences further, Table 6.1 provides a useful summary.

**Table 6.1** Differences between managers and leaders

| Managers ... | Leaders ... |
| --- | --- |
| ... need to get it right first time | ... have the capacity and tolerance for experimentation |
| ... tend to use logic and rationality | ... are able to be creative and use intuition |
| ... need clarity and simplicity | ... demonstrate their tolerance of ambiguity and complexity |
| ... use their ability to manage the present | ... are able to manage into the future |

*Source*: Adapted from Blackwell, 2003

## Working *with* a manager

Working 'with' a manager is different to working 'for' a manager. The subtle change of term implies that you are taking back control, that you have some personal power in working with the change you have been asked to engage. In essence, it is using your skills of leadership on your manager! The key to this is ensuring you don't play their game, but rather, that you play *the* game together.

Remember that the discussion of 'management' is that it is 'top-down': management is 'done' to staff. Also recall the discussion about the various threats. Consequently, trying to engage with a manager who has a high level of responsibility and years of practice is difficult if you use the same strategies as they do. However, in understanding that management is outcome orientated, that results need to be achieved, you are in a position to work with them. Chapter 8 discusses goal setting, and you can use the strategies in this chapter to negotiate successfully what needs to be achieved and when. Your manager should respond positively with your SMART(ER) targets as it demonstrates what will be achieved and how. You are providing something that is 'measurable' and will satisfy their outcome-orientated mind. Of course, be sure that you are the one who sets your own goals ... again we will discuss the reasons for this later in Chapter 8. There again, you may not have the confidence to negotiate your targets: this is where Chapter 4 on confidence, Chapter 10 on self-talk and Chapter 11 on mental imagery will all help.

In negotiating the targets, you are also demonstrating that you are self-motivated and self-disciplined, elements any manager would welcome. To this extent, if they see that you can manage yourself, they can focus their attention on others they may view as 'underperforming', while you get a chance to 'polish your halo'. (Indeed, Thorndike's 'halo effect', 1920, is something to capitalize on – this is where, if you can demonstrate your positive attributes, people will tend to perceive these attributes with you more often.) Related to this, however, is ensuring that you can keep up your commitment and achieve the targets you have set. If you are losing motivation, refer to Chapter 3.

There may be times when you need to put yourself forward more forcefully. Although we would always advocate non-confrontation, being 'assertive' is different.

## Assertiveness

Assertiveness is a communication skill which enables you to say what you want, when you want; providing and justifying your perspective. Furthermore, it helps avoid being used or manipulated by others.

Assertiveness tends to be seen as a 'defensive' approach, whereby if someone asks you to do something you do not want to do, you can 'speak up' and provide your opinion. One way of viewing assertiveness is in considering what it is not. An assertive person is different from an aggressive person and, similarly, is not a passive person. The assertive person is in between.

Aggressive communication is where a person does not really care about another person's thoughts or feelings. Their behaviour tries to influence others and does not take account of the individual. This is akin to 'bullying'. The passive communicator adopts the 'anything for a quiet life' approach. To this extent, they will engage with what is asked as they see this as a better option than confrontation. Yet assertiveness is the 'middle path'. This is where they will acknowledge another's perspective while respecting their boundaries, yet remain true to themselves and be defensive if required. As you may appreciate, being assertive relates to having confidence and self-esteem as discussed in Chapter 4. It is therefore, a positive construct.

Everyone has the ability to be assertive, indeed each of us use our assertiveness to different extents in different situations. One situation where you respond passively may be dealt with assertively by another person, and vice versa. Being assertive however means that you:

- acknowledge your right to express yourself fully;
- acknowledge that you are unique;
- acknowledge that you are in control of your own decisions;
- acknowledge the rights of others in relation to the previous points!

 **Activity 6.2**

In your journal, make a three-column table with the following headings:

- Aggressive
- Assertive
- Passive

Consider people you know (or from the media) who could be listed in each category.

What attributes/strategies does each of the groups employ?

Consider a time when you were 'assertive'. Note down the situation and how you reacted.

Consider a time when you were 'passive'. How could you have responded differently?

Perhaps one of the key reasons why people find it hard to be assertive is because it makes them feel guilty, in that they may be putting the other person out. Of course, this is made worse if the other person is purposely making them feel guilty! Indeed, the influential author, Manuel J. Smith originally wrote his 'Bill of Assertive Rights' in *When I Say No, I Feel Guilty* in 1975. These are listed as:

- You have the right to judge your own behaviour, thoughts and emotions, and to take the responsibility for their initiation and consequences upon yourself.
- You have the right to offer no reasons or excuses for justifying your behaviour.
- You have the right to judge if you are responsible for finding solutions to other people's problems.
- You have the right to change your mind.
- You have the right to make mistakes – and be responsible for them.
- You have the right to say, 'I don't know'.
- You have the right to be independent of the goodwill of others before coping with them.
- You have the right to be illogical in making decisions.
- You have the right to say, 'I don't understand'.
- You have the right to say, 'I don't care'.

There are a number of strategies that can be used to help develop your assertiveness, detailed in Table 6.2. The key is to practise these, perhaps using them alongside mental imagery (Chapter 12) or self-talk (Chapter 11) to enable you to put them into practice when required. Indeed, you may want to role play these with someone you know. For example, let's assume you have been asked to attend an additional parents' group meeting at short notice (see Table 6.2).

Keep in mind that the important aspect about assertiveness is to ensure you know what you want first and that, as with any skill, it takes time to develop. It may be worth considering a 'catch-all' statement in the first instance that provides you with time to think about the request, and in turn, time to develop your response. For example, you may use the term, 'Thank you for asking me. I will get back to you when I have checked my diary'.

## ⌇ Reflection

Over the next week, keep in mind the situations that you could deal with assertively. Make a note of these in your journal. Identify how you dealt with the situation and the strategies you used. If you were not as assertive as you would have wanted, how could you have handled the situation differently?

**Table 6.2**  Assertiveness strategies

| Strategy | Description | Example |
|---|---|---|
| Saying 'no' | One of the hardest words to say ... especially if you are so used to saying the opposite! | 'I would love to attend the parents' meeting but I have a deadline for Monday, so I will have to say "no"' This could be followed with: 'Perhaps if you give me enough warning I may be able to make the next meeting.' |
| Basic assertion | This is a statement where you clarify your position. | 'I have an appointment at 5 p.m. so I need to leave at 4.30 p.m.' |
| Empathy | This is where you acknowledge the thoughts and feelings of another person while approaching them with your thoughts or feelings. | 'I appreciate that you need to find someone to attend the meeting at short notice. Unfortunately I am unable to attend as I have another important commitment.' |
| Broken record | Where you 'replay your message' continually as a person attempts to get the required response. Keep in mind what it is you want and stick to this. Your assertion can become stronger if needed, although if you start too strong, you may appear aggressive. Using the same phrase over and over will help reinforce that you are unable to commit to a request although be sure not to change your mind. | 'Thank you for the invite. Unfortunately I have an assignment due on Monday and will not have the time this week.' This is a 'gentle' starter. Let's assume the conversation continues and each time the same request is made about attending the meeting. 'I have told you numerous times I do not have the time to commit this week.' Obviously you would not start with this assertion! |
| Fogging | Staying calm when criticized. This will remove the 'power' over the comment. To some extent, the person making the comment wants you to agree to overpower you, so in part, you agree with the comment, yet turn it to your advantage through making such comments as: 'You probably have a point, in fact sometimes I think so myself!' Fogging thus 'shrouds' the comment, adapting to what has been said without disagreeing outright. | 'Thank you for pointing out that I never seem to attend meetings. I fully acknowledge your contribution and shall endeavour to attend a future meeting.' |
| Negative assertion | This is where you agree with the parts of the criticism that may be true, or raise your own criticism before anybody else has the chance. Again, this removes the sense of power. You may agree with the | 'You are right, I seldom attend additional meetings.' |

*(Continued)*

**Table 6.2**   (Continued)

| Strategy | Description | Example |
|---|---|---|
| | comment but this does not mean you have to adapt your behaviour should you not wish. | |
| Consequence | This assertion notifies the person of the result of their action. | 'If you continue to ask me to attend the parents' meeting, I will have to reschedule my appointment and may miss the next staff meeting.' |
| Negative feelings | This enables you to highlight your feelings to another person due to their actions. It is based on: When you ... , I feel ... | 'When you keep asking me to attend meetings in my own time, I feel frustrated as I have other commitments which are equally important.' |
| DESC | The acronym DESC was originally developed by Sharon and Gordon Bower. It stands for: Describe: the situation completely and objectively. Express: your thoughts and feelings about the situation. | 'Thank you for asking me to attend the meeting at short notice ...' 'If I commit to attending, I will not have time to plan for next week thoroughly ... ' |
| | Specify: what you would prefer to happen. Consequences: explain the positive outcomes if the course of action is followed. | 'I would prefer to have been given more notice about the meeting as I could have then adapted my working week ...' |
| | Perhaps explain the negative outcomes if the action is not followed. | 'As a result, if I attend I will not be fully planned for next week. If I do not attend, I will be able to commit 100 per cent to the week.' |

 Case study

The Transtheoretical Model (TTM) of Behaviour Change (Prochaska and DiClemente, 1983) was developed to explain how people change from unhealthy to healthy behaviour (originally in smoking cessation). For the purpose of this chapter, the principles are transferable. Essentially, the model suggests that people undergo change over a period of time and experience different cognitions at different stages in the process (which is why the model is also known as the 'Stages of Change' (SoC) model).

Prochaska and DiClemente propose that people move through a set of pre-defined stages in a cyclical fashion (Diagram 6.3), at different rates and sometimes, with a relapse to the previous stage. These stages are:

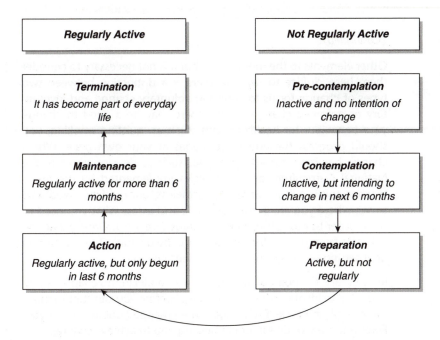

**Diagram 6.3** Stages of Change (adapted from Prochaska and DiClemente, 1983)

- Pre-contemplation. The person is inactive and has no intention to change, even if they know the risks associated with not changing (the 'I won't' stage).
- Contemplation. The person is inactive but intending to change over the next six months. They may have had a health 'scare' but hasn't started to begin the healthy behaviour yet (the 'I might' stage).
- Preparation. The person has started to effect change, for example, by buying a pair of running shoes, joining a gym, or has thrown all the cigarettes away (the 'I will' stage).
- Action. The person started the 'new regime' within the last six months and is actively getting on with it (the 'I am' stage).
- Maintenance. The person has being performing the 'new regime' for longer than six months and has integrated it into his or her routine (the 'I have' stage).
- Termination. This stage does not mean that the person stops the routine. Rather, it means that it has become part of daily life (the 'it's part of my life' stage).

*(Continued)*

*(Continued)*

Other elements to the model exist, but it is not necessary to consider them here. Suffice to say that there is a distinction between two types of change for us to consider: voluntary change and involuntary or enforced change. Where there may be a need to change your behaviour for health reasons, such as, quitting smoking, you should progress through these stages at your own pace. Where change has been forced upon you, such as developments in the National Curriculum, or new policies implemented by the head-teacher, this is a little harder. Nevertheless, our guidance would be to see where you are in the SoC cycle and assess what you need to do in order to move through each stage (we are assuming that you will start from the contemplation stage by default). The chapter on goal setting will help you to implement change.

In summary, the point of introducing the model in this chapter is that you need to identify your current 'stage' before you can start to move on through the cycle. Each stage is then mapped out in front of you. Foresight is a wonderful tool in helping you to achieve change.

## Key issues in facilitating change

A number of issues need to be in place to ensure that colleagues engage successfully with change. The acronym CRIF is one we have developed to ensure the minimum factors are considered in implementing change:

- *Confidence*: do colleagues have the confidence that the changes will bring benefits to the school?
- *Relevance*: can staff see the reason for the change, now? In the future?
- *Implications*: how will the change process affect all involved? The students, the staff, the parents, and so on?
- *Feasibility*: are the resources in place to support the change?

Although CRIF is useful as a 'checklist' to consider when facilitating change, the W5H1 (who, what, why, where, when, how) questions can help in the planning stages for change. For example: *what* is the proposed change; *why* is the change needed; *when* does the change need to be implemented; *who* are the people responsible for bringing about the change and who will be affected; *where* will the change have the greatest impact; *how* will the change be put into practice? (Feel free to adapt the questions as you see fit.)

So far we have discussed the nature of change, why it may come about, and how change should be embedded. Although you may not be

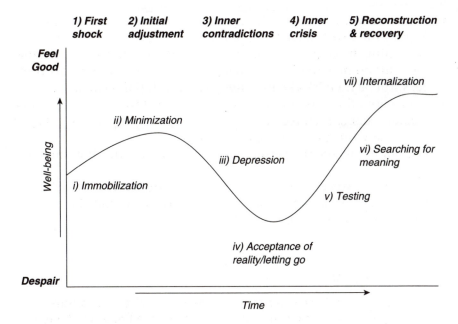

**Diagram 6.4** Kübler-Ross's 'five stages of grief' (adapted from Kübler-Ross and Kessler, 2005)

responsible for leading change at the moment ... you soon will be! However, it is the personal impact of change that affects everyone psychologically, to which we will now turn our attention.

## The psychological impact of change

- All change results in adjustment: this may be adjustment of working patterns through to adjustment of how you perceive the world. Adjustment, however, creates disharmony through having to internalize, and accept, this change.

An alternative model, widely used in counselling, was developed by Dr Elisabeth Kübler-Ross. She originally developed her 'five stages of grief' model in relation to counselling those who were bereaved. Yet since its development, the model has been applied to encompass wider-ranging situations, indeed where anyone is facing change on a personal level, for example, physical or emotional trauma, redundancy, financial burdens, and so on. We have provided the model here to help understand the personal reactions you may experience in relation to change (Diagram 6.4). The stages are:

- Denial: refusing to accept the situation as a defence mechanism.
- Anger: either with themselves or others.
- Bargaining: seeking a compromise as a solution. It must be noted that the solution may not be sustainable. One way to consider this is the 'let's still be friends' scenario after a relationship has ended.
- Depression: this acts as a form of acceptance of the impeding reality. Acknowledging such feelings and allowing them to happen is key to progressing through this stage.
- Acceptance: where the person has come to terms with the situation.

The important aspect to note from working through this model is the various stages you may find yourself going through and the order in which these present themselves.

 Reflection

Consider Kübler-Ross's five-stage model in relation to a situation you may have experienced. This could be the break up of a relationship, moving away from home, coping with a physical injury which has prevented you engaging fully with an activity you enjoy, and so on.

Although both models help to identify and, in turn, understand the process of change, they do not really offer guidance on how best to work with the various stages. Working through the various strategies in this book will certainly help you engage with the various stages, however.

One model which does identify specifically how we can react to change and how to work with the various stages, is 'the change cycle'.

## The 'change cycle'

In understanding the impact of change, it is important to identify the various psychological stages people pass through. Craine (2007) calls this 'the change cycle' (Diagram 6.5).

Fundamental to the cycle is that if change needs to be implemented and you know 'resistance is futile' (for example, it is an initiative you have no say over), then moving through the 'no' zone to the 'go' zone as quickly as possible is required. Thankfully, Craine provides strategies on how to engage with this on a personal basis and in helping others to similarly engage. This is summarized in Table 6.3.

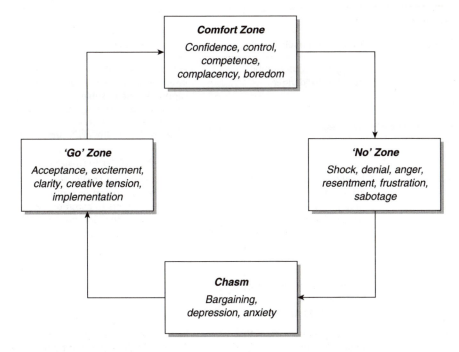

**Diagram 6.5** Craine's 'change cycle' used with permission from Craine, K. (2000) *Designing a Document Strategy*. Hurst, TX: MC² Books, http://www. document_strategy.com

**Table 6.3** Moving through the 'change cycle'

| Zone | To assist yourself | To assist others |
|---|---|---|
| Comfort zone | Appreciate where you experience ease and comfort, where you feel 'protected'. Recognize situations which cause tension, frustration or stagnation and where growth could occur. Generate a development plan for the situations you would like to change. (Refer to Chapter 8 on goal setting.) | Help others appreciate the process and nature of change. Help others understand that change can be positive. Identify where change has occurred and how this has led to success.<br><br>Assist others in developing plans for change. |
| 'No' zone | Recognize your feelings in relation to the change. Acknowledge your feelings. Recognize why change needs to occur in order to develop an existing process. Use cognitive restructuring (Chapter 10) to perceive | Provide others a rationale and context for the proposed change. Ensure others are aware of the various stages for the proposed change. Identify with others how the process of change will result in future success. |

*(Continued)*

**Table 6.3**   (Continued)

| Zone | To assist yourself | To assist others |
|---|---|---|
| | changes as 'opportunity' opposed to 'danger'. | Acknowledge that others may feel insecure about the change. Try to support where possible. Facilitate a goal setting process to identify targets and monitor progress. Ensure the goals are developed together for joint 'ownership'. (Refer to Chapter 8). |
| Chasm | Identify what you want to achieve from the proposed change. Obtain the necessary information and support required to equip you to work with the proposed change. Ensure you remain positive throughout the process by avoiding negative comments from others. | Ensure targets are continually monitored as agreed with others. Encourage others to communicate in order to share their information and concerns and successes. |
| 'Go' zone | Take control over issues that require action. Identify areas outside of your control. Discuss these with others. Visualize how change will be implemented positively. (Refer to Chapter 12.) | Review the goal-setting process. Ensure that those affected by change feel a sense of self-determination. (Refer to Chapter 3.) Identify where change has been adopted and the results from this – successes, innovative practice, and so on. Ensure continued support as required. |

*Source*: Adapted from Craine, 2007

## Wisdom from the ancients

In Chapter 13, we discuss 'flow' or 'being in the zone' … indeed the chapter you have just read could be termed, 'going with the flow'. By this, resisting change will only create disharmony; it is necessary to understand the change before you can engage with and eventually accept the change. An analogy to this may be found within the *Tao Te Ching*, the classic, Eastern philosophy writings (from which we used a previous verse for defining 'the greatest headteacher'). Chapter 76 notes that all things in life are soft and pliable, yet in death are dry and brittle. Consider a willow tree in a storm and an ancient oak tree. Which of these will persevere through being 'flexible'? To this extent, remaining 'flexible' in times of change is important to your continued success in teaching. Just remember, if you remain flexible in times necessitating change, you will be following the guidance of the ancients!

## One-minute summary

The only certainty is the uncertainty of change. Yet in understanding where the change has come from (for example, social, economic, technology, and so on), how it may affect people (threats to authority, power, territory and influence), and the nature of change (innovation, growth/expansion, contraction, diversification) it is possible to engage more effectively with change.

Resistance to change is natural and should be expected, however this is where a leader of change would be preferable to a manager of change. In facilitating change, CRIF (confidence, relevance, implications, feasibility) needs to be considered as a minimum, together with the W5H1 questions.

Associated with change, assertiveness has been discussed in learning how to deal with those who may impose change and how to present yourself so you are effectively heard.

The psychological impact of change needs to be considered in relation to the experiences you may feel. The change cycle provides advice on how to deal with change going from the 'no' zone to the 'go' zone as quickly as possible.

Ultimately, by being flexible and responsive to change, you will excel within the teaching profession. The key word is *adapt*.

## Short-term strategies for the here and now

- Consider the W5H1 questions for the proposed change. Can each of these be answered? If not, seek advice on how they could be resolved.
- Consider the stage you may be going through in relation to change. Are you in a 'no' zone, or a chasm? Understanding the level will help you identify the following steps. Work through Table 12.2.
- Consider how you can take control over a change situation. This relates to aspects discussed in Chapter 3 on motivation and Chapter 8 on goal setting.
- Identify the way in which the proposed change may be affecting you emotionally. If change is having a significant impact on you, it would be worth seeking counselling. Arranging an appointment with your general practitioner would be the first stage; alternately you may have a counselling service where you study, or within your local education authority.
- Practise the following self-talk phrase (Chapter 10) to enable your assertiveness: 'I am always able to express my personal rights and feelings' or 'I am the best judge of my thoughts, feelings and behaviour'.

## Mentoring issues

Discuss with your mentor the impact of proposed changes and how he or she may have coped with change and adapted professionally.

 Further reading

Bridges, W. (2004) *Transitions: Making Sense of Life's Changes*. New York: Perseus Books.
This book has been published for over 25 years and is a practical guide on dealing with change.

Kotter, J. (2006) *Our Iceberg is Melting: Changing and Succeeding Under Any Conditions*. New York: Macmillan.
This is written as a fable about a colony of penguins bringing to light a number of aspects the author is known for in relation to change management.
The topic of 'change' is usually discussed in relation to associated topics, for example, stress. To this extent, please refer to the further reading in Chapter 5.

In relation to the 'grief cycle', you may want to explore the following websites:

www.ekrfoundation.org
www.elisabethkublerross.com

## Answer to the reflection

It may actually surprise you to find that the quote is over 2500 years old and was written by Lao Tzu in China. 'Headteacher', however, has replaced the original term 'leader'.

# Section 2

## Physical issues

Although the following section consists of only one chapter, it is paramount to the book in that a 'healthy body equates to a healthy mind'. As such, if the body is not in tune, this will have a negative impact on the psychological strategies we discuss in this book. Furthermore, we are sure you are aware that teaching is a physical activity! You can be on your feet for eight hours or so during the day. Consequently, the section examines a number of related areas to ensure continued health and optimum performance in the classroom.

# 7

# Fitness to Teach: a Healthy Body Equals a Healthy Mind – Nutrition, Hydration and Health

'It is good practice to seek help from experts outside of one's own field'.

In producing this chapter, we have enlisted support from our colleague, Annie Lambeth, from the University of Worcester. Annie is an expert in Sports Nutrition, providing guidance to clients both through our Human Performance Laboratory and through our Motion and Performance Centre.

Her advice is the basis for the guidance provided in this chapter.

## Introduction – fitness to teach

According to the Education (Health Standards) England Regulations (2003) and *Fitness to Teach* (DfEE, 2000), teachers need a sufficient standard of health and physical fitness to enter and remain in the teaching profession. As such it is recognized that it is a demanding yet rewarding career, although if a teacher's health is jeopardized, their employment may be terminated. To this extent, ensuring your long-term health and fitness is a key component of your career.

Although it is many years since we engaged with our final teaching practice, it was a memorable time of absolute exhaustion! The routine for 10 weeks involved waking at 6 a.m., a quick bowl of cereal, a full day in school, back to plan lessons and prepare resources for the following day which would normally mean getting to sleep at midnight. Lunch consisted of a sandwich and the evening meal perhaps another sandwich due to lack of time and energy to prepare a decent meal. All these 'nutritious' meals were washed down with copious amounts of coffee. In summary, nutrition was questionable, dehydration was paramount, sleep was limited and exercise was non-existent. Needless to say, this was not the best way of 'surviving' and we would hate to think what the long-term implications are for sustaining our 'fitness to teach'.

While working full-time, teachers may be tempted to grab a quick bite to eat on the run, or want a quick fix of coffee and a biscuit from the staffroom. Food and water tend to be given lower priority during the working week, though it must be remembered, they are the body's 'fuel'. You would not dream of driving to work with insufficient fuel or water, so why should your body be any different? In the first part of the chapter we will discuss the importance of adequate hydration or fluid intake. If you are dehydrated, your brain will not function optimally and you will probably have a headache. The second part of this chapter provides some advice to help you eat appropriate, nutritionally balanced foods, which will help you prepare for and get through the week. In the final part of the chapter, we go on to discuss how exercise and physical fitness influence your performance in the classroom. Finally, the issue of sleep (and lack of it!) is discussed. The chapter provides guidance on these issues and we will guide you in the direction of appropriate support.

Although it could be questioned as to why this chapter has been included, in that it is not psychologically based, the unity of the mind and body are paramount as has been discussed within other chapters, for example on stress, feedback, and so on.

As a precautionary measure, you should consult your general practitioner before embarking on any changes to your existing dietary and fitness habits. The information contained in this chapter is for guidance only.

## Chapter objectives

- Understand how the interplay of hydration/nutrition, exercise and sleep promotes successful teaching.
- Consider reviewing your current healthy living activities.
- Identify strategies to further promote your health.

## Hydration

Hydration is easy to overlook and can cause problems at crucial moments. Dehydration does not affect you immediately, but if allowed to develop it will affect all aspects of your performance, and may do so at the most inappropriate of times. To put this into perspective, *if the human body becomes dehydrated by as little as 2 per cent, physical performance can be impaired by anything up to 20 per cent*. If dehydration levels increase further muscular strength is reduced and perception of effort is increased, which significantly increases fatigue. This is how serious and important fluid intake is. In addition to these physical effects dehydration directly impairs brain function, which slows down the decision-making processes, reduces skill and accuracy, is detrimental to attention and reduces concentration. In such circumstances, we would suggest that you pay particular attention to fluid intake, and make sure you drink as much as possible, even if you do not feel thirsty.

*The easiest way to monitor hydration levels is by keeping a check on urine colour*. We provide a colour chart on the website in order to compare the urine colour with your level of hydration, however the simple phrase *'pee light, all is right!'* summarizes the chart. *The general rule is that the darker and more cloudy the colour and the stronger the odour, the more dehydrated you are*. In checking this, we would assume that a teacher has adopted balanced nutritional eating habits. It is important to be aware that vitamin tablets colour urine quite considerably because the kidneys do not absorb all of the vitamins. It is important therefore, to ensure that checks are done beforehand if you take daily vitamin tablets. The same can be said for taking caffeinated energy drinks. As some teachers show a preference for drinks such as Red Bull, this piece of information is important, since it renders the urine chart useless. *Fluid and food intake directly influences brain functioning*.

One final comment about fluid intake is that *a drink with some sugar and sodium in (check the nutritional information) will be absorbed into the body faster than plain water*. Most sports drinks are specially designed to be the optimal concentration for absorption, but make sure you like the flavour. If you don't like the taste of a drink you are less likely to sip on it, and risk becoming dehydrated.

Activity 7.1

For one day, keep a record of your normal liquid consumption. Plot this on a graph, for example:

| Monday | Time | | | |
|---|---|---|---|---|
| | 6 a.m. | 7 a.m. | 8 a.m. | Etc. |
| Tea | | | | |
| Coffee | 2 x mugs | | | |
| Flavoured water | | | | |
| Water | | | | 1x glass |
| Carbonated drink | | 1 x cola | | |
| Alcohol | | | | |
| Etc. | | | | |

Please note that this is not a scientific activity! Its purpose is to raise your attention regarding your consumption of liquids for hydration during the day.

Total up the number of water/water-based drinks (*not* tea, coffee or alcohol). Next total up the number of other drinks. Subtract the latter from the former. Ideally you should still have a positive number (above zero). Alas, if the only water you have is used for making numerous cups of coffee, you are likely to have a negative number and may be actively dehydrating yourself!

Try to balance this out in the following days to obtain a positive number.

# Nutrition

If you are feeling lethargic during the week, one of the things it makes sense to explore is your eating routine. You may be forgiven for thinking that the role of nutrition is to promote energy, but this is not necessarily the case. There are no 'magical' meals that should be eaten to guarantee success. But, **there are foods that are more, or less, appropriate for a teacher.**

We have known teachers who raise their blood glucose levels by eating sweet foods or taking soft drinks, which are notoriously high in sugar.

This might appear to be the ideal solution: a quick burst of short-term energy to last the day. Although it will indeed raise blood glucose levels for a while, there is also an associated side effect, the 'crash', whereby blood glucose levels take a drop, usually to a point lower than they were to start with. The obvious danger is this so-called 'rebound' effect, which will potentially happen 30–60 minutes after consuming a high-sugar snack. This low blood glucose level and associated drop in concentration, energy and focus is not what you want to occur in the middle of a lesson. Consequently, we would not advocate these kinds of 'quick-fix' snacks, but instead recommend slow-released, slower digesting foods such as muesli bars, cereal bars, low-fat sandwiches, and bananas.

## What to eat?

The first thing we must point out is that there *is no single 'set menu'* that you should adhere to. Obviously, people have different preferences and tastes. So, this section will give you a guide that you can adapt to suit your own needs and perhaps special dietary requirements. The second thing we must point out is that this chapter is *not* about dieting. There is a misconception that dieting is the same as healthy eating. It is not. In eating 'healthily', you can still have 'naughty' foods (although we hate this term), but in considered moderation.

You can start the healthy eating process at any time. However, we would suggest that you ease yourself into it during a half-term break, end of term, or at the very least, during the weekend, when you have a little more time on your hands. You should consider eating fish and chicken rather than red meat, and pasta or rice meals rather than fried foods or take-away. When having pasta dishes, try to go for vegetable-based sauces rather than cheesy sauces which are high in hidden fats. Snack on low-fat biscuits, cereal bars, bananas, fruit and nuts to avoid hunger between meals. Avoid, or at least reduce your intake of tempting snacks such as pastries, cakes and chocolates, so you can maximize your intake of energy rich foods without taking in too much fat. Use the weekend to prepare nutritionally for the week. At worst, it will help you through Monday. At best, it will become part of your healthy eating plan and should help 'the new you'!

### Reflection

No doubt your school has adopted the healthy schools initiative. Question your relationship with food and whether this adheres to current dietary advice (five-a-day, eat a rainbow, and so on.) Do you practise what the initiative preaches for the students? (In the past we haven't!)

**Activity 7.2**

For one week, keep a record of the food you eat, for breakfast, lunch, dinner and any snacks you have. Try to be accurate *and honest* with your estimates.

The purpose of this activity is to raise your attention regarding your food choices.

Look at this food diary and see where you can make changes, based on the information we have provided.

## Exercise/physical activity

The general rule of thumb is that overall physical fitness, acquired through appropriate and regular exercise regimes, is undoubtedly of benefit to all. If you have the luxury of being able to schedule exercise into a hectic teaching week, this is an excellent way of keeping fit.

At this point, we must clarify the misperception about exercise. It is not 'sweat, pain and gyms'... it is 'any form of physical activity' (within reason), for example, gardening, walking to the local shop as opposed to taking the car, housework, washing the car, and so on.

The teaching day is the culmination of all the planning and preparation. Lesson plans, resources, books, handouts, and so on come together to form a coherent package for the day. This should be no different for you, the teacher. Nutrition, hydration, and energy levels, through exercise and fitness, should be at their optimum.

Psychologists generally agree that exercise and mood are linked. Put simply, if you are feeling 'low', the evidence suggests that you will feel so much better after a period of exercise. What better way go into a teaching week than on a 'high'? It is the 'feel-good' factor that rewards us.

You probably have a whole host of questions now. When should you participate in physical activity? How much should you do? When should you stop? When should you step down a gear? Of course, this will be different for all of us. There is no single piece of guidance on fitness regimes. Our advice, beyond this chapter, would be to consider seeking a fitness assessment. There are many specific books on the market and it is not our intention to provide specific guidance on fitness regimes here. The references at the end of this chapter will guide you.

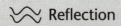 Reflection

You may exercise regularly, or the mere thought of it might make you shudder. Whatever your relationship with exercise, is there anything you can do from day to day to ensure you are even more active? For example, this may be parking in the space furthest away from the school so you have to walk further. Perhaps there is an activity you can take up? Remember to always get the advice of your general practitioner before embarking on an exercise programme.

 Activity 7.3

For one week, keep a record of the exercise or physical activity you undertake. Try to be accurate *and honest* with your recording. You should also keep a record of how you felt afterwards. Did you feel energized? Did you feel that things became clearer in your mind? Did you enjoy it?!

The purpose of this activity is to raise your attention regarding your physical activity levels.

Look at this physical activity diary and see where you can make changes, based on the information we have provided. Avoid 'overdoing it'!

## The importance of a good night's sleep

Sleep … how often do you think about it? Is it one of those humanly habitual aspects that you seldom think about? We may think about 'going to bed' and remembering to set the alarm clock, but is that it?

Considering we spend a third of our lives engaged with this activity, *sleep is a fundamental aspect of our health* – we think about nutrition, exercise and hydration but do we necessarily think the same way about sleep? Indeed, poor quality sleep can lead to many psychological conditions, for example irritability, lack of concentration, longer reaction time, anxiety and depression. Physically, lack of sleep can put you more at risk of obesity and infections. However, good quality sleep has been found to be beneficial for learning and memory, boosting the immune system, contributing towards cardiovascular health and rejuvenating your skin! Ultimately, though, it increases your decision-making and productivity, meaning that you can do the same amount of work in less time, or work smartly as we like to say. Yet we tend to stay up late, or get up early to work longer which seems to be a self-defeating paradox.

How much sleep should you have? This is like asking the question, 'How long is a piece of string?' Studies have suggested that some adults should sleep for eight to eight and a half hours, although this could be broken into a six-hour main sleep and an afternoon 'nap' for a couple of hours, although let's face it, when would we ever get the luxury of a two-hour afternoon nap! However, a 10-minute 'micro-nap' may help to rejuvenate you if you are flagging.

 ## Activity 7.4

Explore your sleep patterns. If you normally go to bed at 10 p.m. and wake at 6 a.m., you may want to try exploring different ways of resting. Perhaps go to bed at midnight and wake at 6 a.m., then have a nap for a couple of hours from 5 p.m. onwards. Needless to say, it is best to explore different sleep patterns during your holidays – we certainly wouldn't recommend it during term time!

## Sleep deprivation

Building up a sleep debt is akin to building up financial debt … at some point it needs 'paying off'. In the short term, you can repay a couple of nights of little sleep by catching up and extending sleep over the following few days. However, if you continually get little sleep during the week and try to make this up over the weekend, it will have an overall impact on your quality of sleep. For longer periods of sleep deprivation, you can make it up with longer periods of sleep over a few days, before your body comes back into balance. Ultimately the message here is explicit: ***don't assume that you can get by on a few hours of sleep and expect to give your best teaching performance***. Similarly, don't assume that you need to 'claw back' *all* of the lost sleep. The brain 'catches up' on REM sleep (rapid eye movement) and slow wave sleep, both of which are considered to be vital for successful brain function.

 ## Activity 7.5

For one week, keep a 'sleep diary'. Try to be as accurate *and honest* with your recording. Approximately how much sleep did you get each night? Based on your performance the next day, was this amount of sleep enough? Would you benefit from a 10-minute 'micro-nap' at lunchtime in your classroom?

The purpose of this activity is to raise your attention regarding the amount of sleep you have (and the amount of sleep you may need).

Look at this sleep diary and see whether you need to make changes, based on the information we have provided. The key is getting the balance right for you.

## What can prevent quality sleep?

You may well be able to identify aspects that prevent you from sleeping. For example, watching television, or playing a computer game prior to turning in for the night can prevent you 'dropping off' due to your mind 'still buzzing'. Also, ensure that you leave work alone for at least an hour (and preferably in a different room to the one in which you will sleep) before you intend to go to sleep, for the same reason.

Similarly, caffeinated drinks, or aspects in the environment (for example, is it too hot or too cold?) can inhibit your slumber. Alcohol is another potential 'danger area': although you may fall asleep initially, alcohol interferes with the natural progression through the different stages of sleep. You may find that you wake at 3.00 a.m. and are not be able to get back to sleep. Ironically, sleeping tablets have a similar effect of interfering with the natural progression of sleep patterns, tending to keep the person in 'non-REM sleep' (if you are taking medication to 'help' you sleep, you might consider the underlying reasons, implement a coping strategy from this book and no longer have cause for the medication ... although you should of course discuss this with your GP). Perhaps you have just eaten a large meal and will spend the next few hours digesting it, something that is less than 'restful'.

The following section of this chapter explores aspects to aid sleep.

## What can facilitate quality sleep?

Needless to say, ensuring all the factors that prevent quality sleep are eliminated is a starting point. Exercise or physical activity a few hours before turning in can help, as can having a pre-sleep routine.

If the worst comes to the worst, we hope that reading this book doesn't send you to sleep! We have, however, listed below a number of 'environmental' issues and strategies to help your overall sleep quality:

- Unwind mentally: try reading or listening to music.
- Try to keep electronic gadgets out of the bedroom: the electromagnetic fields of televisions, computers, and so on are known to impede sleep.

- Close the curtains. The darker the room, the more likely your brain will be able to synthesize melatonin (low levels of melatonin are believed to impair the sleep–wake cycle).
- Ensure the temperature is 'right': try to keep on the cool side. Lower than 23°C (75°F) but not lower than 12°C (54°F).
- Try to ensure your bedroom is as dark as possible: use lined curtains or an eye mask.
- Consider your bed! You will spend a third of your life in it and most beds are kept for 10 years or more. To this extent, get advice on buying the best bed for you.
- White noise: this is a randomly generated sound, very much like the 'buzz' of an untuned radio (although with DAB nowadays, again this may be a sign of technological progress … or our advancing age!) You can search the Internet for various white noise downloadable files and transfer this to an MP3 player.
- Avoid animals sleeping in your room: there is nothing like 'Fluffy' snuggling up to you and keeping you awake as they enjoy their slumber. We even know of a teacher that kept a pet hamster in his bedroom, who liked nothing better than a 2 a.m. 'workout' on its exercise wheel!
- Consider aromatherapy or essential oils: benzoin, German and Roman chamomile, jasmine, lavender, sandalwood and ylang ylang are all known to help sleep. (Note – please seek expert advice before using such oils as you may be sensitive to them!)
- Try the exercises from Chapter 9 on relaxation before you go to sleep.
- Try the exercises from Chapter 10 on self-talk to instruct your mind that it is now time to 'switch off'.
- Keep pen and paper next to your bed: if any distracting thoughts wake you, you can make a note. This stops the thought being cycled in your mind as you know 'it is there' and you can deal with it when awake.
- Age-old sleep promoters: for example, warm milk, a hot bath, and an established bedtime routine – these are things that are tried and tested!

 Activity 7.6

Complete an environmental audit of your bedroom. Try to limit the potential sleep inhibitors, while promoting the sleep facilitators.

Furthermore, consider getting a plastic box in which you prepare a 'sleep kit'. This may include an inexpensive MP3 player which only has your white noise, relaxation scripts, or relaxing music … something robust which you can stick under a pillow. You may also want to include an eye mask, aromatherapy oil, a postcard with your self-talk phrases, pen and paper, and so on.

## One-minute summary

This chapter has explored the interplay between hydration, nutrition, exercise and sleep. Think of these topics as each sharing a corner of a square. If one of the 'corners' is missing, one cannot have a square. If one of the 'corners' is 'damaged' or 'weak', the box may collapse.

Adequate hydration is important for all cells in the body. It is especially important for brain function. Cognitive processing relies on water and is impaired when fluid levels drop. Equally, nutrition provides the necessary 'fuel' for our journey, whether it is a vigorous team game in PE or whether it is a long afternoon in class during the latter part of the school term. Exercise, or should we say physical activity, may at first appear to be 'energy-sapping', but is important in providing the 'lift' that will help you to cope with the challenges ahead. If you still see it as 'energy-sapping', think in more positive terms. Exercise will take your mind off the worry issues, or it will help you to deal with them more effectively due to increased oxygen levels in your brain. It will also promote restful sleep, the 'fourth corner' of the square.

## Short-term strategies for the here and now

- Look back at the chapter on stress. If you identified any 'stressors' in your life, ask yourself how you could address these through hydration, nutrition, exercise and sleep.
- *Hydration*. Are you drinking enough during the day? Is this the correct fluid? Keep a log as suggested in Activity 7.1.
- *Nutrition*. Begin to think about 'power foods'. By this, we mean foods that will keep you going. Avoid doing too much at once. Try not to revamp your whole eating regime in one step (you will probably set yourself up to fail). Start by cutting out *some* of the sugary snack foods identified in Activity 7.2, but remember to replace them with a substitute snack because you will still be feeling 'peckish'.
- *Exercise*. Consider planning a 20–30-minute walking route around the area in which you live and set a target of achieving this three times per week (you might also purchase a pedometer to record the amount of steps taken), with a longer route at weekends. You *will* feel better for doing so, even if you don't feel like stepping out of the door.
- *Sleep*. Remove all traces of 'work' from the bedroom. The bedroom is a place of comfort. It is there (for the purpose of this book) to help you to 'recharge your batteries' in readiness for the next day. You will not be able to do this if there are reminders of 'work' around you. Close the study door and enter the bedroom. You will have separated work from sleep and should already be making life easier. Avoid checking emails or working on the computer just prior to retiring for the night. Take some time to unwind before retiring for the night.

## Mentoring issues

The areas discussed in this chapter are perhaps personal to you and you may not want to discuss your sleeping routine with your mentor! Yet general discussion about keeping healthy, specifically if anything is jeopardizing your health in relation to work, needs to be considered and discussed with your mentor, for example, if due to excessive work-loads, you are not getting the sleep you require to function effectively in the classroom.

## Further reading

There are numerous resources available on the areas discussed in this chapter. Exercise is a personal venture – one person may prefer a solitary activity, another may prefer a group-orientated activity. Whatever your preference, remember to seek medical advice first, and then explore for relevant resources around your chosen activity. Similarly, nutrition and hydration are discussed through many different resources.

A couple of introductory texts relating to exercise and nutrition are:

Denby, N., Baic, S. and Rinzler, C.A. (2005) *Nutrition for Dummies*. Chichester: John Wiley and Sons.

Schlosberg, S. and Neporent, L. (2005) *Fitness for Dummies*. Chichester: John Wiley and Sons.

In relation to sleep, the following text is fascinating and authoritative, yet accessible:

Horne, J. (1988) *Why We Sleep: The Functions of Sleep in Humans and Other Mammals*. Oxford: Oxford University Press.

# Section 3

# Psychological skills training

The previous chapters have discussed how psychology (and physiology) influence our performance in the classroom. In these chapters, we have continually made reference to the following chapters which discuss how to develop skills and strategies to ensure your success in the classroom.

Chapter 8 examines goal setting and how to engage with this effectively to motivate and monitor your performance. Goal setting is something we tend to use with our students and perhaps seldom use personally. This chapter consequently examines the benefits of setting personal and professional goals, and how to maintain these.

Chapter 9 identifies ways in which we can use relaxation after a hectic day or week in the classroom. Relaxation is more than collapsing in front of the television. The chapter discusses a number of strategies we have used with teachers which include physical and mental relaxation.

Chapter 10 explores self-talk and cognitive restructuring. We continue to have an internal dialogue throughout the day, yet often this can work against us. How can your inner voice be turned into one of the most powerful psychological tools available? How can you reprogramme your thoughts to ensure you meet with continued success? We would like to put a health warning on this (and the next) chapter as together, they may influence your life in numerous positive ways!

Chapter 11 discusses mental imagery. This develops from the last chapter whereby we identify ways in which to use strategies of 'playing things in your mind' to your advantage. Again this is similar to the reprogramming in the previous chapter.

Finally, Chapter 12 looks at combining all of the skills and strategies to become mentally resilient … how to maintain your performance throughout the duration of the term, or the year, when previously you may have felt like quitting.

# I Have 101 Things to Do ... What Do I Attempt First? Goal Setting

## Introduction

As teachers, we tend to be experts at setting goals for our students ... yet how often do we apply the same goal setting to our professional life to ensure we continue to strive for success?

Setting goals is an ideal way of progressing in teaching. Consider the pathway of headteachers, inspectors, advisers who have all progressed from their teacher-training days. So, is goal setting the key to success? No! *Achieving* those goals is the key to success. In our experience, teachers often report setting goals that are either unrealistic, overly vague or they are so distant that they become demotivating. Examples of such goals include: 'I want to complete all my weekly planning over the holidays', 'I want to write all my reports this morning', 'I want to have a life and not work every weekend' … we're sure you get the picture.

## Chapter objectives

- Understand the importance of goal setting and how it relates professionally.
- Distinguish between outcome, process and performance goals.
- Consider the strategies for setting relevant SMART/SMARTER goals.

## What is goal setting?

Goal setting is a technique used to assist people in meeting targets at some point in the future. It is a 'how-to-get-there' resource which can, for example, help teachers to set targets in order to reach a certain level of expertise. Setting appropriate, specific goals helps to improve performance and enables levels of motivation in achieving these goals to continue. Essentially then, it is target setting. We must clear up one issue at this point. Goal setting involves setting one's own targets and is very effective in helping us to achieve the goals we set. In reality of course, other people may set targets for us. Often we are unable to negotiate or change these targets, so we have to find ways of achieving them. Goal setting is a way of moving closer to achieving those targets. You might not like the target set for you, but need to find a solution to achieving it. Goal setting offers that solution.

 **Activity 8.1**

Before reading any further, list five or so targets in your journal, that you would like to achieve, or have been advised that you must achieve in the next academic year. These are your goals. Keep this list safe. You will need to refer to it later in the chapter.

## Which perspective: outcome, performance or process goals?

Psychologists suggest that there are three different types of goal. It is important that you are aware of the difference between these types.

## Outcome goals

As you might expect, **outcome goals are based on the end product of a performance: on its outcome**. By the very nature of outcome goals, the frame of reference is a comparison between your performance against targets, or ensuring your students reach their targets, or perhaps comparing yourself with another teacher's performance, and so on. You are comparing yourself on outcomes, outcomes which may well be beyond your control. In teaching, outcome goals are prevalent in terms of reaching targets. A teacher who may have set their class the target of all achieving a required grade and is teaching effectively may still fail to reach their set goal. Not only is this demotivating but it also does not take into account any success that has been achieved, for example, a student who has made exceptional progress from their starting point, yet who may still not have achieved the set target.

## Performance goals

Performance goals may be seen as diluted versions of outcome goals. In essence, they **are related to a teacher's performance regardless of the outcome**. The comparison is between your performance now and your performance last week, or last month. An example of a performance goal might be to ensure all work is completed within the school week, so that the teacher has their weekends free to get refreshed (something that was perhaps unachievable a month ago). We would argue that performance goals are preferable to outcome goals, since they relate directly to a teacher's development. So, we may be the worst teachers in the school, yet if our performance is improving, we are achieving success!

A good use of setting performance goals is to modify an existing performance goal to see if you can push it that little bit further.

## Process goals

Arguably the most appropriate kind of goal setting involves examining the process of teaching, the 'flow' required to get students learning in an effective, smooth manner. **Process goals are, therefore, about 'how it feels'**. Think of a time when everything was working well in the classroom, a time when you were in your element, where the lesson was effortless, enjoyable and exceptional (enough of the alliteration!). Consider why this was the case. What did you do to facilitate this successful scenario?

For every element of teaching, it should be possible to set a process goal so that you can get the most out of, yet expand, your teaching experience. You can do this by working out what information you will need to perform the process successfully. For example, you may have utilized a new teaching technique from a staff development session, or tried a new technique for getting the class in order. Perhaps you have adopted a new method of planning or assessing. Essentially, it is something that 'just feels right'. The key is to strive for the 'correct feel' and to take this knowledge into each aspect of your career. So, you should aim to set goals on the basis of 'doing the job' rather than on the end product or outcome. If you take care of the process the outcome will take care of itself.

### Activity 8.2

In your journal, note down in your own words the difference between outcome, performance and process goals. For each, note a couple of examples you could demonstrate. You may also want to discuss these with your mentor.

## Is setting process goals the simple solution?

Although the idea of setting process goals might seem convincing, the simple answer is, *'No!'* Teachers may enhance performance by employing a combination of goal-setting strategies. Such a tactic would be ill-advised until you are sufficiently familiar with goal-setting techniques. Such techniques require investment of your time and effort before they can be adapted to suit changing situations.

## How does goal setting work?

Knowledge of how goal setting may exert its effect on performance will help you to understand how to set effective goals and how goal setting can be utilized in directing your attention, channelling effort, persistence, and developing new strategies of learning how to overcome challenges. We will explore each of these in turn.

### Directing or focusing attention

It is important to direct attention towards a specific goal. Teachers who do not focus on specific goals usually find themselves floundering and their attention easily distracted from the task at hand. You will perhaps have experienced the feeling of, 'So many things to do ... which one first?' then you end up failing to complete any of them in a particularly focused manner. This might include not paying adequate attention to the timing and pace of your lesson. If attention is directed at ensuring a steady pace and ensuring you leave time for a plenary and clearing away before the bell, you can focus on this as a goal. Essentially, the teacher is breaking down the overall task of teaching into *small, manageable 'chunks'* which can be developed with practice; a sort of, 'I need to do X and Y if I want to do Z' approach.

### Channelling effort

Having focused your attention on a specific goal, as in the example above, you then need to make a concerted effort to achieve that goal. On its own, therefore, directing attention is not enough. *Active effort* is also required in achieving the goal. You need to evaluate how you are going to achieve the goal.

## Persistence

Having directed attention and mobilized effort in pursuit of the goal, the next step in the process is persistence. In attempting to achieve the goal, it is of no benefit for a teacher to direct attention and mobilize effort for the first few lessons of the day. It is not enough to persist for the three days of the week. *Persistence means having the stamina to keep going for the duration of the week.* It is the endurance element in order to reach the set goals which enables a teacher to achieve success.

## Developing new strategies of learning to overcome challenges

Having directed attention, mobilized effort and persisted in the activity, you are finally able to develop new strategies of learning. This ensures that you do not become 'stale' and shows adaptation to the ever-changing circumstances. Think of this as being similar to evolution. No species remains the same but rather, constantly adapts to the changing environment. *A teacher should be striving to adapt to different situations, take opportunities when they emerge and look for the most appropriate strategy for the situation.*

Whether you achieve your goals may also depend on the following.

## Ability

We have hinted at ability above. Your ability is an obvious point for considering whether you can actually complete the task successfully. Do you have the relevant knowledge, experience or resources to hand? Perhaps reflecting with your mentor can help improve your ability on a particular aspect. Avoid setting goals that are beyond your ability. Be aware, however, that as you develop, your ability may also increase.

## Commitment

It is vital for a teacher to be committed to achieving the goals that he or she sets. If commitment is absent, there is very little chance that the goals will be achieved, at least in part because the desire must also be missing. This is more difficult when targets have been set for you. We like the idea of differentiating between targets (set by others) and goals (set by ourselves to meet others' targets). By differentiating in this way, you can 'take ownership' because you are striving to achieve your own goals, which will, in turn, meet others' targets.

## Feedback

Feedback is a vital element of goal setting. Feedback provides the teacher with a way of *evaluating whether the goal has been achieved or not*. Of course, there are objective measurements that are of use in establishing whether a goal has been achieved, such as discussions with your mentor, observations, and so on. We would also argue that subjective information is relevant in terms of feedback, but only if it can be quantified. For example, we might ask you to rate the 'feel' or 'success' of a particular lesson on a scale of 1–10, where 1 is poor and 10 is excellent, as discussed below.

For example, imagine a teacher has been asked, 'On a scale of 1 to 10, how did the lesson on introducing the concept of gravity go?' Let's assume the answer is a 3, and of course, this is unique to that particular teacher on that particular occasion. We would then ask the teacher to explore ways in which they might approach this task in a different manner, in order to improve on the 3 rating. This could be through ascertaining what students already know about gravity through using concept maps, perhaps discussing in greater detail why things fall down as opposed to up, or additional practical activities on dropping different sized objects, and so on. Although this is subjective, it does offer a way in which a teacher can measure their performance.

## Task complexity

The complexity of the task may influence the effectiveness of the goal. Setting a particular goal of completing all your short-term planning for the term may be unrealistic as you will have to be flexible and accommodating to your students' needs as they develop: your planning may be aimed at the wrong level. It is important therefore, when setting goals, that they are *realistic, given the complexity of the task*.

The setting of inappropriate, outcome goals can lead to problems with self-confidence, anxiety and satisfaction. The more confident you are, the greater the likelihood of achieving the goal. Psychologists call this *'self-fulfilling prophecy'*. If you believe that you will fail, you *will* fail. If you are confident that you will achieve, then you will. Additionally, each performance has a certain amount of anticipated satisfaction attached to it. *When goals are achieved, satisfaction increases, confidence grows and motivation to achieve the next goal remains strong.*

Regardless of the theoretical perspective one adopts, goal setting remains one of the most important techniques in psychology in helping teachers to develop skills and achieve success. The effective use of goal setting is imperative in this development and, it is to this that we will now turn.

## 〰 Reflection

Consider a time when you may have set a personal or professional goal. Did you achieve it? We tend to remember the goals we achieve and forget the ones we don't. As such, if you can remember a goal you didn't achieve, was this due to your ability or commitment, lack of feedback on progress or the complexity in achieving the goal?

Perhaps consider a goal you may currently be working on. Do you think it will need revising in light of what has been covered so far in this chapter?

## Effective use of goal setting

From our experience in working with teachers, it is apparent that a lack of appreciation and understanding of goal setting has led teachers to set inappropriate goals, or to think about their performance in the classroom in the wrong way. This is quite normal. When asking teachers what their personal goals are, we tend to find that they do not set personal goals but their goals are linked in some way to the outcome of the class. We frequently get responses such as 'to ensure all my students reach x level in y subject'. In itself, this is all very well. However, the difficulty is that not all factors are controllable for your students in order for them to achieve a set target. By approaching goal setting from a different perspective, the attainment of others is not as important as the process of achieving personal and professional growth ... which ultimately will ensure attainment as a by-product. Once a teacher understands this, their performance should improve and students will make the required target as a 'side effect' or consequence of the process. In our opinion, this is implicit in the way 'inspirational 'teachers, such as Phil Beadle, the award-winning, unorthodox yet effective 'super-teacher', approach their lessons. Telling teachers not to focus on student outcome is among the hardest things we do. Telling you that improving your own performance through setting appropriate goals is like putting money into a savings account; at some point in the future it will provide you with everything you need.

## Guidelines for writing your own goals

Various types of goal-setting systems exist in psychology. However, most involve three logical, progressive stages: preparation and planning, education and acquisition, and implementation and review or follow-up.

### Preparation and planning

It is important for you to assess your abilities and needs. For us, a teacher's input is essential and will guide our assessment. A useful method of keeping motivation levels high is to *set wide-ranging goals*, so that you can work on different elements at different times. It is important to plan to help achieve the strategies you have put in place, so that you are aware of whether progress is being made. For example, we may agree to use goal setting to:

- overcome motivational or confidence problems;
- aid the development of teaching technique and/or mental preparation;
- help you through a programme of injury rehabilitation;
- assist you in recovering from staleness or burnout.

**Activity 8.3**

Look back at the targets you listed in Activity 8.1. Plan and prioritize your goals by making a list. Pick no more than three to work on first, before moving on to the next three, and so on.

## Education and acquisition

When carrying out a goal-setting strategy, it is necessary to organize regular meetings with your mentor to monitor performance in relation to the set goals. Some people advocate working on a single goal at one time although we would suggest that you may be in a position to work on more than one goal during a particular period. Again, the responsibility for appropriate goal setting rests on collaboration between the teacher and the mentor.

After initial preparations, it becomes possible to observe and monitor progress and overall confidence in a teacher's ability. As goal-progression or goal-achievement data is collected, a picture builds up and this may serve to motivate you to continue with the programme.

 **Activity 8.4**

Set a deadline for the future. This may be a week, a month or a term, depending on the goals you have listed. Identify what types of evidence you need to collect in order to assess your progress towards meeting the goal.

## Implementation and review

It is important that you identify relevant procedures for the assessment of goals. If you do not know how the procedures work, there is little chance of success. Throughout the process, the mentor should provide appropriate support and encouragement wherever progress towards goal achievement is taking place. You should set a date for the review of your goals. It is important to reflect on progress, achievement or reasons for not meeting your goals.

In setting a date, it is necessary to be mindful of the time frame associated with different goals. Goals may be short, mid or long term. Of course, this distinction is specific to each teacher. What we consider to be a mid-term goal for one teacher, may be a long-term goal for another. We will now outline each type of goal below.

**Activity 8.5**

Reassess your progress at the deadline, or review date. Mark off the goals that have been achieved. If any goals have not been met, reflect on why this might be and consider revising the goal for a follow-up review.

## Long-term goals

These are your ultimate goals, the things you desire most from your career. Long-term goals can cover a single year, or your entire career. You set the boundaries yourself and your long-term goals relate to your own perspective on time. However, this poses a problem in terms of keeping the motivation alive for the duration of the goal-period.

## Mid-term goals

Mid-term goals act as a way of keeping motivation levels alive. They serve as a focus at a closer point in the future. How do you know whether you are progressing towards your long-term goal? You know because you have set and achieved a mid-term goal. Mid-term targets should be clear and should be set in relation to long-term goals. For example, if you have set a long-term goal linked to the end of a year, then your mid-term goal will perhaps be after a term. If, however, your long-term goal is a five-year plan, then the mid-term goal might be assessed at some point during the third year.

## Short-term goals

Short-term goals are, again, relative to mid- and long-term goals. They serve as a focus point in the near future. You do not have to wait for too long before a short-term goal can be assessed for progress. In keeping motivation levels high, *short-term goals should provide manageable, regular opportunities to achieve success*. In setting a personal target, rather than an outcome-based goal, you can concentrate on your own strategy, rather than becoming a pawn in others' games. Having achieved this short-term goal, you should then consider setting a new short-term goal for the next time frame.

# Common goal-setting problems

Without appropriate guidance, it is easy to fall into the trap of failing to achieve the goals that have been set. If progress is not monitored, as we have mentioned, there will be an increasing likelihood that goals will not be achieved. Indeed if goals are not achieved, motivation may be diminished and performance impaired as a result. Not only should goals be monitored, but they should also be revised or readjusted as necessary.

*If you have not achieved the goal set, then refocus, or 'dilute' it so that you can achieve it*. It may be that the original steps towards the goal were simply too large. Keep this statement in your mind: 'If I chip away at my performance, I will get where I want to be at some point.'

It may be that the goals set are too general or not measurable. If you are unable to measure achievement towards the goal, how do you know whether you have reached it or not? We will discuss these points in greater depth, under the section on SMART targets. Similarly, if you set too many goals, you may not be able to achieve all, or any of them in the timescale you have set for yourself.

Finally, individual differences play a role in goal-setting problems. We would not ask you to compare your fingerprint with ours and tell us which one is the best. In the same way, the goals you set for yourself should not be related to what other people are doing or can do. We would, however, expect you to set a goal that might ultimately send you on the route to success … which indeed is among our foremost reasons for writing this book!

## An introduction to SMART goal setting

SMART is an acronym for a technique that helps psychologists and teachers set appropriate goals. It stands for *Specific, Measurable, Action-oriented, Realistic and Time-phased* (although as with most acronyms, there can be variations on a theme). We shall take each element in turn.

### Setting SPECIFIC goals

It is important when goal setting that you identify exactly what goal you wish to achieve. It is no use saying, 'I want to be a good teacher.' This is too general. Instead, you might wish to ensure that all your lessons utilize an effective plenary. If you achieve this, you can take the opportunity to re-adjust and consider other goals. If you focus on a specific goal, then a number of specific goals can make you that good, if not great teacher.

### Setting MEASURABLE goals

Having set a specific goal, it is vital that some form of measurement is used to evaluate whether or not the goal has been attained. This is perhaps the most awkward aspect to set in terms of identifying an appropriate measure. Think of a piece of string. If we ask you to measure the string without using a ruler, the likelihood is that you will overestimate or underestimate its length. If you use a ruler, there is an absolute measure that can be relied on. Absolute measures are not always possible in goal setting. Nevertheless, the aim is to strive towards precise, observable measurement wherever it is available. A measurable goal is therefore quantifiable and, as such, acts to tell the teacher whether it has been reached.

## Setting ACTION-ORIENTED goals

As one might anticipate, action-oriented goals are goals that highlight something that needs to be achieved. An action-oriented goal is not thinking about an activity, but rather is about taking steps that will change something.

## Setting REALISTIC goals

If your goals are unrealistic, there is little chance of achieving them, motivation may diminish and performance may become impaired. Setting a realistic goal will provide a 'light at the end of the tunnel', something that is within your grasp and will assist you in getting to where you desire to be. It would be unwise, however, to set goals that are so easily reached that achieving them becomes meaningless. This high-lights the importance of setting realistic, yet challenging goals. If there is little in terms of challenge, you are unlikely to receive satisfaction from the task. In writing this book, we set ourselves the goal of writing 1,000 words a day. We consider this to be realistic and challenging, with-out being so difficult that we cannot meet the goal. As a result, we have been successful thus far and get a sense of satisfaction every time we achieve our goal for the day. If we set our sights beyond this word count we may not reach the daily goal and this may lead to despondency. If, on the other hand, we set the goal at 500 words a day, we doubt if we would get any satisfaction and you would not be reading this book!

## Setting TIME-PHASED goals

There is little use in setting goals without a deadline for review. This essentially is what we mean by the term, time-phased. A time-phased goal must be accomplished by a particular deadline, or 'target date'. Again, if you set a deadline that is too short, the goal may not be achiev-able, so it is important to remain realistic about your expectations for accomplishing the goal. Of course it is possible that you may have dif-ferent goals with different deadlines. So, you may have a time-phased goal linked to performance during the forthcoming lesson, but you might also have a time-phased goal of achieving consistency over a number of lessons this half-term. There is, therefore, an element of crossover with target dates.

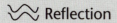 Reflection

Start to consider SMART goals for your development. Just make a mental note of these at the moment as we will come back to setting them shortly.

## Even SMARTER targets

It has taken a few years but the SMART acronym has been extended to include Exciting and Recorded. Exciting targets ensure that you meet them sooner than bland targets. Recorded relates to writing the goal somewhere that you can see it every day as opposed to filing it away and forgetting about it. We will discuss this further in a moment.

We like the idea of recording goals but disagree that they should always or indeed can always be exciting. Sometimes a goal may be bland, yet necessary and there is nothing we can do to alter its blandness. However, if it is exciting, you are more likely to achieve it, because striving to achieve it is enjoyable.

## Additional practical guidance on setting goals

The psychology literature provides additional practical advice for effective goal setting. Issues include setting performance and process goals, setting goals for complementary areas, recording goals, and goal-commitment and support. We will briefly outline each issue below.

### Setting performance and process goals
It is good practice to set both performance and process goals. Indeed, it is acceptable to set outcome goals, but these should be of secondary importance. Performance and process goals should provide you with the necessary requirements to achieve the desired outcome. You should concentrate on your own performance and the process you go through to achieve that performance.

### Setting goals for complementary areas
It is quite common for teachers to set goals only for the day-to-day job. We would, however, advocate that you set goals for all aspects of life that relate to your teaching. As teaching is likely to take a considerable 'chunk' out of your week, ensuring you are able to balance other dimensions of your life is crucial! You should also consider whether to set goals in relation to themes discussed elsewhere in this book. While you might have a National Curriculum-based set of goals on one sheet of paper, a set of exercise/physical activity goals on another sheet of paper, a set of confidence-related task goals on a third, a set of time management goals on a fourth and … the list is almost endless.

Consider earning your salary but frivolously spending it to 'reward' yourself for a job well done. This may lead to debt (if your student loans aren't enough!) which in turn will add pressure to your life and potentially undermine all the good work you have done so far. Setting goals for spending time with family and friends, or for exercise and entertainment, and so on are also vitally important.

## Recording goals

Recording goals is vital to progress. The academic year is long: if we ask you in May, to cast your mind back to a lesson in January, could you remember all aspects of what happened? This is unlikely! Consequently, we would encourage you to keep a personal log relating to your goals. What were the goals for each week? Did you achieve them? If not, why? What were the readjusted goals? Did you achieve them? It then becomes possible to look back over the year, review progress and reflect on the implications in advance of next year. Examples of ways in which to record goals can be found later in this chapter.

## Goal-commitment and support

It is important that teachers 'buy in' to the idea of goals and their effectiveness in improving performance. The teacher must show commitment to achieve. All people associated with the teacher are in a position to foster that commitment by providing support wherever possible. It is of no use whatsoever for the mentor and teacher to work on a goal-setting programme, only for the headteacher to override the programme and instead set unrealistic, outcome goals. If everyone is aware of the goals, achievement becomes more likely.

## Feedback

As we have pointed out elsewhere, feedback is a vital element in goal setting. The mentor is responsible for evaluating progress on the goal-setting programme and providing feedback where appropriate. Feedback may sometimes be seen as 'criticism' depending on how it is delivered. However, it should be viewed as a means of communication that enables the teacher to refine their performance.

 **Reflection**

Consider the way in which feedback is given. What is the difference between positive, constructive feedback and criticism?

 **Activity 8.6**

Having reached the end of this chapter you should now be able to set your own SMARTER goals. These may vary considerably from the way in which you wrote down the goals in the earlier activities in this chapter. Your task is to put these newly acquired skills into operation. The form at the end of the chapter should be used to list these goals.

We have included a summary information sheet at the end of this chapter that we give to teachers during discussions on effective goal setting. We find it useful because it provides sufficient information to enable teachers to refer to it quickly and easily during their hectic schedules.

## Dealing with 'imposed' goals

From time to time, you may be set goals over which you have had little, or no, control. By this, you may have been asked to complete a task which is not necessarily part of your workload. If you are assertive enough to give a resounding 'no' at the outset, this would be beneficial. If you have reluctantly agreed to the goal (because you were caught 'off guard' or thought that it would make you 'look good') will you continue to question your decision, or see it as unfair? Of course, there are always 'shades of grey' with such issues! You may not want the goal that has been set for you, and you know that refusing to engage with it will have an adverse effect. If we analyse the situation, it is possible to identify ways to deal with this (see Diagram 8.1).

As discussed in Chapter 3 on motivation, the area of self-determination is characterized through feeling competent (having the skills), the feeling of autonomy (being in control) and the feeling of relatedness (how you engage in the social setting). If one (or more) of these areas is threatened, you may well feel uncomfortable with what has been asked of you. For example, you may be asked to step in to cover a lesson for another teacher. You may well have the skills; you may well understand that this will be looked upon favourably; however, you may feel that the control over your 'free time' has been taken away.

So how best can you deal with such situations? The key is to identify what is causing the personal disharmony. Once this is identified, you can then take the necessary steps to regain control as identified in the suggestions below:

- Lacking the competence – discuss that you may not have the skills or confidence necessary to complete the task. Perhaps you could work with somebody on achieving the goal.
- Lacking autonomy – look for a way in which you can make the goal personally meaningful, or a way in which you can assert your autonomy while working with the goal.
- Lacking relatedness – identify how you could work with others in order to reach a satisfactory conclusion to the goal.

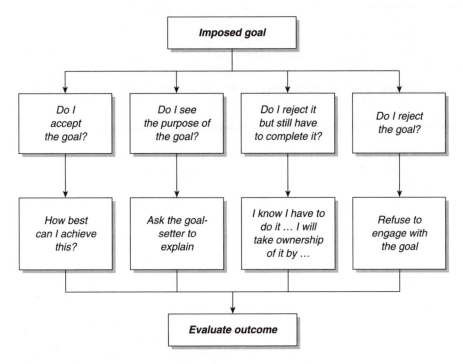

**Diagram 8.1**   Possible ways of dealing with 'imposed' goals

 Activity 8.7

Consider a time when you were asked to complete a goal that was 'imposed' by another. What were your feelings? What was the resolution? Re-evaluate the situation in relation to the three areas of self-determination. For this, note down in your journal strategies in which you could have reasserted control over such 'imposed' goals.

## One-minute summary

Effective goal setting is a fundamental skill in order to progress successfully within teaching. To this extent, it is important to focus on the type of goal you are aiming for. Is it one or more of the following?

Outcome – focusing on the end product.
Performance – focusing on your actual performance.
Process – focusing on how it feels.

Setting goals is useful as it helps direct and focus your attention, in turn channelling your effort and ensuring persistence. As a product of achieving the goal, you may also have developed new strategies for learning to overcome challenges. However, any goal is dependent on your ability to achieve that goal, your commitment, obtaining feedback so you know how well you're progressing and, finally, task complexity – if the task is too complex, can it be divided into smaller goals?

The key message is that a written goal somehow becomes formal. It is there for you (and others if you wish) to see. You have therefore committed yourself to set about achieving it. Setting SMART or SMARTER goals is perhaps the best way to proceed.

## Short-term strategies for the here and now

- Do you have any definitive goals, or is it that you just want to survive? Goal setting can help you make better use of your time and keep you more focused so not only are you surviving, but you are also thriving as you are receiving feedback as to the excellent job you are doing.
- Set one or two short-term goals for the coming week. They could be anything – perhaps even something 'routine' like ensuring by the end of the week you can have a weekend to yourself. In order to do this you may need to consider when would be best to complete your planning for next week and when would be best to complete your marking, and so on.
- Use the SMART planner at the end of this chapter to structure this goal. As a worked example:

  o (S) Complete next week's planning by Friday.
  o (M) All lessons for all five days will be planned and prepared.
  o (A) Planning sheet and lesson plans need completing.
  o (R) The planning can be achieved after the team meeting on Tuesday.
  o (T) Monitor progress on Wednesday. This will allow two days to prepare resources.

## Mentoring issues

The three stages of preparation and planning, education and acquisition, and finally implementation and review would be worth rereading as they specifically highlight issues to discuss with your mentor.

Your mentor may have already negotiated targets with you. You may want to re-evaluate these with your mentor so that they adhere to the SMART framework as discussed throughout this chapter.

Remember that feedback is important: as such, your mentor should be able to inform you of your progress towards achieving these goals.

## 📖 Further reading

There are numerous books on goal setting that are available, ranging from the theoretical to the practical. As we have noted in this book, a balance of both, theory to contextualize the practice, is essential. Consequently, we feel that the advice given in this chapter is an ideal start to goal setting. The following books and papers are listed to supplement your understanding.

Hamson-Utley, J.J. and Vazquez, L. (2008) 'The comeback: rehabilitating the psychological injury', *Athletic Therapy Today*, 13(5): 35–8.
This paper explores the relationship between physical and psychological components in the rehabilitation of athletic injury. For our purposes, however, it discusses how goal setting can provide an element of control in the recovery process (and the principles would be no different if you are recovering from a non-sporting injury). It also discusses the link with mental imagery, to promote healing, decrease pain and improve self-motivation.

Lee, S.H., Palmer, S.B. and Wehmeyer, M.L. (2009) 'Goal setting and self-monitoring for students with disabilities: practical tips and ideas for teachers', *Intervention in School and Clinic*, 44(3): 139–45.
This paper (written for the US education system) gives practical guidance to teachers on self-monitoring, through goal setting, for students with disabilities. Nevertheless, it provides practical examples, tips and strategies on how the teacher can support students in striving towards their goals. In our opinion, it would be wise to read this paper and apply it to your own goals, in order to gain an appreciation of how to support your own students, when helping them to set goals.

Mayne, B. (2006) *Goal Mapping: How to Turn Your Dreams into Realities*. London: Watkins.
This book discusses the principles of success before progressing to discuss 'the goal-mapping technique' which uses words, pictures and symbols to 'programme' your goals.

Wilson, S.B. and Dobson, M.S. (2008) *Goal Setting: How to Create an Action Plan and Achieve Your Goals*. 2nd edn. New York: Amacom.
The book encompasses such topics as dealing with obstacles, being assertive, delegating and time management in order to achieve your goals. The book is a practical toolkit with worksheets, and so on.

| Date | |
|------|---|
| Focus | |

| Specific | |
|----------|---|
| Measurable | |
| Action-orientated | |
| Realistic | |
| Time-phased | |

| Date for review of goals | |
|--------------------------|---|

# Take a 'Break': Relaxation

## Introduction

It is quite common, in many walks of life, to hear the phrases, 'Just relax', 'Chill out', 'Don't get so tense' or any variations on these themes. On the surface, we would have to agree that this is good advice for teachers. Once upon a time, schools used to have a place of such sanctuary to relax ... the staffroom! Yet such spaces (if they still exist in your school) may be far from relaxing!

In teaching, however, the implications of not being relaxed are potentially severe, culminating in excessive stress-loads or potentially leading to an instantaneous poor decision with personal and professional repercussions. So the general advice would be to do just that, 'Relax'. Yet very few people are ever shown how to relax properly. If you do not know how to do this it is not possible without some form of training. ***To dispel a common myth, relaxation is not simply about taking a few moments to unwind, listening to some music, taking a walk and so forth.*** Of course, such activities can be considered 'relaxing', but relaxation is about so much more than this. Various techniques exist and we will discuss these in this chapter. Chapter 5 on emotion, mood and stress links nicely with relaxation, as does Chapter 2 on concentration and attention. It is important to note that relaxation training should not be thought of as a simple technique that can be learnt quickly. Rather, it may take longer than teachers anticipate. The key to success is that it should be carried out in a systematic, progressive manner.

## Chapter objectives

By the end of this chapter and completion of the activities, you should be able to:

- Define relaxation and understand the differences between physical and mental tension.
- Understand that relaxation requires engagement to produce the required effects.
- Identify how anxiety, stress, attention and concentration relate to relaxation.
- Develop and practise some relaxation strategies.

### Activity 9.1

- Divide a page into four (or use separate pages of your journal). In the first box put the word 'relax'. In the second box put the word 'stress'. Consider as many synonyms (alternate words) as you can that may be related to each of these.
- At the bottom of these first two boxes, write a sentence which defines each of the key words, 'relaxation' and 'stress'.
- In the third box, write down as many activities as you can think of that help you to relax.
- In the fourth box, write down any stressors related to your teaching that you can think of.
- Finally, identify the three most significant relaxing activities and the three most significant stressors from your list.

# What is relaxation?

Explaining relaxation at this point would be like our telling you the ending of a new movie that you are desperate to see, or the outcome of a book you have bought but have not yet found time to read. You need to experience it for yourself! Nevertheless, as the chapter unfolds, it will become clear that **relaxation is so much more than the state of 'relaxing'**. In practical terms, **relaxation is an important tool teachers can use to minimize stress in potentially stressful situations**.

Psychologists generally agree that relaxation is seen as a way of overcoming issues relating to over-arousal and anxiety. As explained in Chapter 5, we all need a certain amount of anxiety in order to function properly. As you stand in your classroom waiting for the day to start, you should not be too relaxed but then neither should you be too anxious. This chapter is about finding the balance, or reducing anxiety of some form or other.

# How does relaxation work?

In our dealings with teachers, we are often asked the question, 'How does relaxation work?' Our response is usually to answer with a question, 'What do you want to relax?' What we are trying to establish here is whether the person is experiencing somatic anxiety (physical tension) or cognitive anxiety (mental tension): although they both relate to each other, establishing the cause can ensure correct guidance for either somatic relaxation or cognitive relaxation. It is more important, however, at this stage, to discover their own perceptions of what they need, before we make our decision about their requirements. The same applies to you. While it gives an indicator of where to head next, you must obviously bear in mind that you may be misguided in terms of your requirements, and we would explore this in more depth.

The differences between somatic and cognitive relaxation are distinct. They can be categorized as muscle-to-mind relaxation and mind-to-muscle relaxation, respectively.

# Physical tension: somatic or 'muscle-to-mind' relaxation

The premise underlying somatic relaxation is that the mind cannot be anxious in the absence of muscle tension. So, if there is no tension in the muscles, then the messages going back into your brain must be saying that there is no need for anxiety. If you reduce tension in your muscles, the signals going back to the brain will tell you that you are no longer tense.

The key here is that you need to know what signs to look for and we will cover these shortly when we outline four basic, yet really effective, relaxation techniques.

## Mental tension: cognitive or 'mind-to-muscle' relaxation

Cognitive relaxation acts in the opposite direction. Rather than the muscles providing the mind with information about tension, it is negative thoughts that are causing anxiety and these thoughts may then lead to muscle tension. If the teacher trains his or her mind to relax, then the muscles in turn will become relaxed.

---

If you flip a coin, it *cannot* fall on both sides at the same time. If you feel mentally or physically relaxed, you *cannot* be anxious.

---

 Activity 9.2

In your journal:

- List as many indicators as you can think of which would indicate physical (somatic) tension.
- List as many indicators as you can think of which would indicate mental (cognitive) tension.

## The importance of breathing!

Each of the techniques mentioned below involve mastery of breathing. It is not enough to simply outline these techniques out of context. Rather, it is important to understand that appropriate breathing is a necessary requirement and to receive guidance in correct breathing techniques. This may sound strange, given that breathing just happens ... a newborn baby can breathe without being taught. You have been doing it for a while now so you must be pretty good at it! As such, breathing is a function of the autonomic nervous system and is controlled without thinking. Indeed, if we ask you now to hold your breath for as long as possible, we will not have to tell you when to start breathing again, it will simply happen after a while. Consequently, *the type of breathing required for relaxation techniques is rather more formal and structured, yet equally simple with practice*. To use an analogy, think of your body as the school's heating system on a cold winter's day. If the boiler has not been used or serviced over the summer, the likelihood that it will break down on that first frosty morning in October is high. Yet if the boiler has been serviced, warmth and vibrancy are spread on that first morning. Similarly, if you service your breathing apparatus, you can now breathe more easily and unlock extra power when needed for your teaching.

During daily life, many of us use *thoracic, or, chest, breathing*. It is superficial and shallow, generally only utilizing the upper section of the respiratory system. Chest breathing is fairly rapid and is associated with the rigours of daily life. In contrast, *abdominal, or deep, breathing* is rhythmic, slow and, as expected, deep. It utilizes the full capacity of the respiratory system. You can feel the difference as you read this section. Does your breathing feel shallow and irregular? Now, if we ask you to take a breath, fill your chest with air, then fill some more and, finally take one 'extra' breath to fill your lower abdomen, you will understand the difference in capacity. When you have filled this 'extra space', hold for the count of three and then slowly and gently release the inspired air to the count of five. *Do this properly three times and we guarantee that you do will feel more relaxed than you did before starting the task.* Having shown that there seems to be an immediate difference, it is now possible to practise deep breathing to feel the benefits.

Whenever you are under pressure, you can use this quick and effective method of 'refocusing' on the task to be done. So, if you are feeling anxious, take a few deep breaths and your tension should begin to disappear. Think of this as the 'sticking plaster' approach to a flesh wound. Ideally, as you will understand through this book, you should not be in a position in the classroom where you feel unready, because your mental preparation will overcome any difficulties. However, if you need to employ 'emergency' measures, they will be at your fingertips so to speak.

Think of the lungs as having three compartments: shallow, middle and deep. As you breathe in, fill each section in turn before you exhale.

## Common relaxation procedures

To recap, the distinction between somatic and cognitive relaxation should be remembered as a quick and effective way of establishing preliminary information about tension and anxiety. We will now discuss four common techniques used to elicit relaxation: Progressive Muscle

Relaxation, self-suggestion (or autogenic training), meditation and listening to your body (or biofeedback). We will then conclude by introducing the idea of an enhanced relaxation procedure, using psychological principles to provide what can perhaps be described as a 'supercharged' technique due to its links with mental imagery techniques discussed in Chapter 11.

 **Activity 9.3**

As you read through the next four subheadings, try to summarize each of these in fewer than 20 words in your journal.

## Progressive Muscle Relaxation

Progressive Muscle Relaxation or PMR, is a muscle-to-mind technique, originally developed in 1938 by Jacobson. Essentially, this technique involves tensing and then relaxing different muscle groups. *If all of the muscle groups are relaxed, then there can be no tension in the body*. As a consequence, any tension in the mind should disappear. It is important that the teacher knows the difference between these two opposing states. Awareness of muscular tension will act as the trigger for the teacher to begin the relaxation technique. Table 9.1 provides practical instructions for PMR. It may help to transfer the instructions into audio format, so that you can play it back and follow the 'verbal' instructions it gives.

When you have mastered PMR, you can dispense with the tension part of the technique. By this, we mean that you can go straight to the relaxation steps, because you have already identified tension. *This is where the benefits occur.* If you are standing in the classroom, with tense shoulders and one minute to go before the morning bell, there will not be enough time to run through the whole technique. Instead, you should simply feel the tension in your shoulders and run through the relaxation step for these muscles. *Within a matter of seconds, you should find that the tension dissipates and is replaced with relaxed shoulder and neck muscles.*

Job done, time to regain focus, hone in to a smooth start to the day and wait for the bell to ring. Some teachers like to incorporate a key word, 'relax' into the technique at each stage, so you can modify the procedure to suit yourself. We will discuss self-talk in Chapter 11, but the use of key words does suggest that links can be made between many psychological skills techniques in order to provide teachers with an effective, indeed 'tailored', adaptation to suit their own specific requirements. Of course, if this relaxation technique works for you,

**Table 9.1**  Instructions for Progressive Muscle Relaxation

Follow each step, by tensing and relaxing each muscle group in turn. You should pay attention to the difference between tense and relaxed muscles. Each step should take approximately 10 seconds.

| Step | Instruction |
|------|-------------|
| 1 | Make yourself comfortable in a quiet environment. Remove or loosen any restrictive clothing. Breathe in deeply, hold and exhale. Do this two more times. You should begin to feel more relaxed. |
| 2 | If you hear any noises, do not ignore them, but focus on inhaling and exhaling slowly. |
| 3 | Begin by tensing the muscles of your lower left leg and foot by pointing your toes. Hold this tension for five seconds and then relax. You can feel the difference between tension and relaxation in your calf and foot. Repeat this procedure once more. Do this for the left leg and then twice for the right leg and foot. |
| 4 | Move on to tensing the left thigh and buttocks. Tense the left thigh muscle and buttocks by pushing down into the floor. Hold this tension for five seconds and then relax. You can feel the difference between tension and relaxation in your left thigh and buttocks. Repeat this procedure once more. Do this for the left leg and then twice for right thigh and buttocks. |
| 5 | Next, tense and relax the left bicep. Do this by bending at the elbow. Hold this tension for five seconds and then relax. You can feel the difference between tension and relaxation in your left bicep. Repeat this procedure once more. Do this for the left bicep and then twice for the right bicep. |
| 6 | Next, tense and relax the left forearm. Do this by making a fist. Hold this tension for five seconds and then relax. You can feel the difference between tension and relaxation in your left forearm. Repeat this procedure once more. Do this for the left forearm and then twice for the right forearm. |
| 7 | Move on to tensing and relaxing the muscles in your back. Do this by arching your back. Hold this tension for five seconds and then relax. You can feel the difference between tension and relaxation in your back muscles. Repeat this procedure once more. Next, tense and relax the muscles in your stomach and chest. Do this by inhaling, holding and releasing. Hold this tension for five seconds and then relax. You can feel the difference between tension and relaxation in your stomach and chest. Repeat this procedure once more. |
| 8 | Next, tense and relax the muscles in your neck and shoulders. Do this by shrugging your shoulders. Hold this tension for five seconds and then relax. You can feel the difference between tension and relaxation in your neck and shoulder muscles. Repeat this procedure once more. |
| 9 | Move on to tensing and relaxing the muscles in your face and forehead. Do this by clenching your jaw and frowning. Hold this tension for five seconds and then relax. You can feel the difference between tension and relaxation in your facial muscles. Repeat this procedure once more. |
| 10 | Mentally scan your whole body for any tension. If there is any, release it by tension and relaxation. |
| 11 | Finally, focus on the relaxed feelings your muscles are now giving you. You are calm and relaxed. |
| 12 | Before getting up, it is important to return to a greater degree of conscious awareness. Count slowly, from 1 to 7, exhaling on every count. As you get closer to 7, you will feel more and more alert. |
| 13 | You should now feel completely relaxed and rejuvenated. |

then there is no reason why it won't work for your pupils. You may decide that a two-minute class relaxation task becomes the norm for your lessons.

## Self-suggestion (or autogenic training)

Autogenic training is a mind-to-muscle technique, originally developed in the 1930s by Schultz (see Schultz and Luthe, 1959). The underlying concepts of autogenic training are the ***physical sensations of 'heaviness' and 'warmth'***. Mental effort is directed towards a particular body part and a sensation of heaviness is produced in that body part. For example, we might instruct you to imagine your right calf becoming extremely heavy. We would then ask you to imagine the right calf losing its heaviness and becoming warm and sun-kissed. After successful practice, we would progress by directing your attention towards 'coolness' in your forehead. The remaining element of this technique is to direct attention towards having a rhythmic breathing pattern and strong, stable heart rate. This technique is akin to self-hypnosis and rests on verbal instruction or internal thought processes. For example, 'My right calf is heavy; my right calf is relaxed and warm; my heart rate is slow and calm; my breathing is strong and rhythmic; and, my forehead is cool.' This technique takes a long time to develop to a high standard and, given that teachers' schedules are usually rather hectic, is not ideal. However, it is available and may prove useful, so the message is to give it a try.

## Meditation

Meditation is a centuries-old (if not millennia-old) technique, aimed at eliciting relaxation. It has perhaps gained a certain stigma in modern society, due to its association with religious experiences, the 'new-age' or cults. To label it in this way would be unfair and one should remember that if it enhances performance, there should be little concern about how it is used elsewhere in society. Indeed, there are numerous academic psychological studies which demonstrate the remarkable benefits from meditation.

The key to meditation is to ***adopt a passive approach. This means that rather than having an active mind, you should practise redirecting your attention towards a cue word***. By focusing on a key word, such as 'calm' or 'relaxed', you are able to let the active thoughts 'wash over' yourself. This is similar to situations where everyone around you has been experiencing stress and you simply 'rise above' the stress, coming out seemingly unscathed. The cue word enables you to do the same in meditation. Table 9.2 provides basic instruction in achieving a meditative state.

Achieving a successful meditative state will take time and effort: similarly it should be practised regularly. It is important that you avoid practising shortly after a meal since the activity of your digestive system will interfere with achieving the relaxation response.

In practical terms, meditation enables teachers to focus or switch attention selectively, when required. It allows for the 'screening out' of unwanted or undesirable information at appropriate moments. For

**Table 9.2** Basic meditation instruction

| Step | Instruction |
|---|---|
| 1 | Find a quiet environment and sit comfortably. |
| 2 | Shut your eyes. |
| 3 | Relax the muscles in your feet and move up through all muscle groups in the body, finishing at your facial muscles. |
| 4 | Focus on rhythmic breathing through your nose, ensuring your lungs are filled with air, through diaphragmatic breathing (ensuring your stomach extends as you breathe in and contracts as you breathe out). Ensure you breathe calmly, slowly and that it is comfortable. Say the word 'calm' as you breathe in and 'relax' as you exhale. |
| 5 | Continue doing this for a couple of minutes initially. Try to extend the time you focus on your breathing up to 20 minutes. (You may want to set a timer prior to the commencement of the meditation.) |
| 6 | When you are ready to finish, keep your eyes closed, sit quietly and let 'active' thoughts return to conscious awareness. |
| 7 | Open your eyes and remain seated for a few moments. Ensure you stand up slowly. If you are feeling faint or dizzy, sit back down for a few minutes. |

*Source*: Adapted from Williams and Harris, 2006

example, consider the situation where you have taught a lesson which perhaps did not go as well as you had wanted, that the pupils just didn't seem to achieve the level of work you wanted them to in order to be prepared for a forthcoming exam. As you take a break before the next class, you replay the lesson over in your mind to try to work out what you could have improved, why did you get it so wrong? At this point, the last thing you should do is focus attention on the problem, or on the time left to overcome it. Rather, your focus should be elsewhere. By selectively attending to your key word of 'calm' or 'relaxed' you are freeing up your mind and enabling yourself to put full attention into the final lessons of the day.

In general, although there are different meditational practices, they all have a common element of *mindfully concentrating on one thing*, whether this is breathing, focusing on one object (for example a lit candle), a repeated sound (like a chant or the Tibetan Buddhist mantra, 'Om Mani Padme Hum' – pronounced ohm mah nee pahd may hung) or a picture (for example, a symbol or mandala of significance).

Psychologists continue to debate exactly how meditation exerts its effects and whether meditation affects performance directly or indirectly. We would tend to think that the effects are more likely to be indirect: meditation has an effect on reducing tension, stress and anxiety, and these in turn appear to improve performance. However, this discussion is of little practical benefit in the classroom. Put simply, if it works for you, use it. If it doesn't, then don't. Also, remember that meditation should not be confused with medication. The former means that a person is taking active control over their situation. The latter means that they may need to read this book!

## Listening to your body (what psychologists call biofeedback)

Biofeedback has been considered to be a relaxation technique. We would also like to think that it is *a way of using signs and signals from your body to check whether your strategies are working* in your favour or against you. In order to do this, you need to be made aware of what to look for, in recognizing the correct signs. In a laboratory setting, this would be achieved, for example, by recording the electromyogram (EMG), skin conductance response (SCR) and heart rate (HR). Yet, such measurement techniques are largely inaccessible to teachers. However, biofeedback devices are readily accessible to us all – cheap (and expensive) heart rate monitors are available in many sports shops, or through Internet retailers. Indeed, we have delivered lectures and classes using these devices, out of curiosity about what our heart rate does during such sessions. Nowadays, we can attune to our breathing and to our heart rate. If we feel tension in our chest as we breathe, that we are not breathing slow deep breaths, then we are probably tense. If we feel our hearts pounding rapidly, then we are not that relaxed (or perhaps we are excited about our verbal ramblings ... even if nobody else is!)

 **Reflection**

Try each of the methods above. Does one stand out as being more suitable for you than the others? In your journal note down the following:

- What method is it?
- Why do you think this method is more suitable for you than the others?
- How can you incorporate this into your everyday schedule?
- When will you set a time to practise this method?
- Where will you be able to practise this method?
- Who could you get in contact with to learn more about this technique?

## When should relaxation techniques be used?

As we pointed out earlier, relaxation techniques should be used to combat muscular anxiety (somatic) or mental anxiety (cognitive). It is vital that you explore your optimal levels of arousal for peak performance. Imagine sitting in the staffroom, prior to the start of the day.

You are running through a deep relaxation exercise and are now in such a state of relaxation that you are no longer ready to carry out the task in hand. As such, we would suggest finding out what level of arousal you need in order to perform successfully. This can be explored through discussion and concentrating on how you feel during the course of the day. If, after a day of teaching you felt you were unable to retain focus or were 'having an off day', we may infer that the relaxation technique was employed at an inappropriate time. We would have to adopt a calculated, although somewhat trial-and-error method of finding the most opportune time to employ the technique. For this very reason, *you should be 'practised' in using relaxation techniques before you need to use them for that all-important visit by the inspectors/tutor/mentor!*

It is, however, possible to keep an eye on proceedings during teaching in order to identify when problems begin to emerge. Psychologists are often experts in using observational techniques, which will enable them to pinpoint various occasions where tension and anxiety manifest themselves through a teacher's behaviour. We observed a teacher gently tapping their hand on the desk waiting for their pupils to quickly tidy up after an art lesson. This sign of tension led to an increasing sense of frustration as the teacher obviously wanted the lesson to end so that the pupils could finish on time. The teacher was running behind schedule and this was making the pupils late finishing the lesson. If this teacher had been successfully practised in relaxation techniques, they would have refocused on what actually needed doing, restoring an organized and methodical clear up, in turn reducing any tension and ending the day in a calm, relaxed way. This is the essence of relaxation techniques. If you only have a matter of seconds to prepare, then you need to be able to use a technique that can be adapted to suit the situation.

It is common, among trainee teachers we have worked with, for them to practise relaxation techniques during the days leading up to a teaching practice and during teaching practice so that they are mentally and physically prepared for a successful and stimulating experience. *The message is quite simple. Identify when it is necessary to relax and find the time and place to carry it out. Relaxation is an important part of a teacher's preparation.* If it is left out or a half-hearted attempt is made, there can be no guarantees that performance will be successful. If, however, time and effort are allocated, the possibilities are limited only by the teacher's confidence and ability.

Next, we would expect you to 'feel' the change to relaxation as you run through the PMR or autogenic technique. We would expect your heart rate to be reduced through your awareness of biofeedback and we certainly would not expect you to enter a 20-minute meditative state just before the pupils come into the classroom.

Case study: Enhanced Relaxation Training (ERT)

This case study acts as a link between relaxation and mental imagery techniques, outlined in Chapter 11. John King, a psychiatrist from Worcestershire developed a technique for use with patients suffering from depression who were referred to him. The technique, which he called Enhanced Relaxation Training (ERT) aimed to reduce or 'improve' the symptoms of depression, by providing patients with a mental simulation of a 'seaside' environment. Essentially, this clever technique involved sounds and smells of the coast, combined with the 'feel' of sunshine, provided by heat lamps. King used mental imagery to underpin these stimuli, by talking his patients through a mental sequence of visual events at the seaside. The result was a mental imagery sequence that was 'lifelike' for his patients. The technique rested on simple, yet effective theory. In the main, people go on holiday to relax, unwind, recover from the stresses of daily life and return feeling refreshed.

King assembled all of the relevant props to provide the context for a holiday in the privacy and safety of his consulting room and was able to manipulate the environment such that he could introduce feelings of calmness and relaxation in his patients. He was then able to make suggestions about how the 'seaside' seemed to be improving their mood and emotional feelings, thus providing these patients with a dilemma: if my mood has improved, how can I be depressed? You will recall a similar argument earlier in the chapter regarding anxiety and relaxation. Of course, we have simplified the situation considerably. However, it is only necessary to highlight the concept of what King was attempting to do.

The message is simply that if you wish to 'get into the mindset' of relaxation, you should put as many 'props' in place as possible. Of course, we do not want you to think that combining mental imagery and relaxation training is only useful for combating depression. Rather, mental imagery may be used to induce relaxation quickly and easily, with the power of verbal persuasion.

 Activity 9.4

From the case study outlined above, what would your 'ideal' escape consist of? What memories are evoked from a time or place where you felt relaxed? Make a note of these in your journal.

- Consider a series of multi-sensory props you could collect.
- Consider how you could collect these props (if you need to download a sound file of waves crashing, or use an audio recorder to record such sounds, and so on).

Having read this chapter, you will begin to realize the significance of anxiety, stress, attention and concentration. Somatic and cognitive anxiety was discussed more fully in Chapter 5 in relation to stress and in Chapter 2 in relation to attention/concentration. If you read each of these chapters again, we would advise you to return to this chapter to cement your understanding of how relaxation is intimately interlinked.

## One-minute summary

This chapter has focused on relaxation, a word commonly used but one which is frequently misunderstood. Relaxation is more than finding a distracting activity and takes time to learn. It is important to learn to relax as this helps to minimize stress in potentially stressful situations. The opposite of relaxation is tension, thus the first aspect is to work out whether you are physically or mentally tense. As the mind and body are integrated, relaxing the one will relax the other. The key is to work out which one has caused the tension.

There are various strategies to enable relaxation:

1. Progressive Muscle Relaxation, where a person tenses and relaxes each of the main muscle groups working from the feet to the head.
2. Self-suggestion (or autogenic training), where a person imagines a part of their body (for example their leg) to be extremely heavy, then light and warm. The exercise progresses to making the suggestion that their heart is slow and calm, their breathing strong and rhythmic, and their forehead cool.
3. Meditation, where a person closes their eyes, relaxes the muscle groups and concentrates on breathing naturally.
4. Listening to the body (or biofeedback), where a person attunes to their breathing and heart rate to provide feedback as to their state of tension or relaxation – if the chest is tense, breathing will not be relaxed, if the breathing is not relaxed, the heart is probably pounding rapidly.

Take time to try out these strategies aiming to spend at least 10 minutes a day consciously relaxing and taking note of the benefits.

## Short-term strategies for the here and now

- Relaxation is more than finding something else to occupy the mind, like watching television – relaxation is a conscious activity.
- Take nine slow, deep, diaphragmatic breaths, concentrating on the in-breath with the word 'calm' and on the out-breath 'relax'.
- Are you physically tense? Relax the mind through concentrating on the breathing.

- Are you mentally tense? Relax the muscles through progressive tensing and relaxing, starting from the feet and working upwards.
- Consider 'mindfulness' as discussed in Chapter 2. You may want to engage with a 'mindful' practice, for example, eating, or breathing.

## Mentoring issues

The way in which you relax is quite personal, therefore you may not want to discuss this with your mentor. You could explore ways of 'switching off' from the job and ask as to their strategies for relaxing.

## Further reading

Crandell, S. (2005) 'Chill out! 23 anti-meltdown tips from top stress experts', *Prevention*, 57(7): 156–201.
As the title points out, this paper provides practical guidance on how to deal with stress. It is very 'accessible'.

Kabat-Zinn, J. (2001) *Full Catastrophe Living: How to Cope with Stress, Pain and Illness using Mindfulness Meditation*. London: Piatkus Books.
Jon Kabat-Zinn's work on 'mindfulness' is currently receiving a lot of attention due to the therapeutic effects it has had. This book can be read as a beginner's guide to meditation and consists of an eight-week programme called mindfulness-based stress reduction.

Ornish, D. and Bodian, S. (2006) *Meditation for Dummies*. 2nd edn. Chichester: John Wiley and Sons.
This book provides a simple, practical overview to a variety of meditation techniques without necessarily being over-religious or philosophical in nature, instead concentrating on the practical techniques. There is something for everyone in here!

## Additional resources

There are a number of 'relaxation' CDs available on the market. On their own, they are less of a benefit but when used in combination with other resources mentioned in this book, can be useful.

Please refer to the website for downloadable relaxation files, where the authors will guide you to a progressive relaxed state.

# 10

## Is Talking to Yourself the First Sign of 'Madness'? Self-talk and Cognitive Restructuring

## Introduction

In the chapter on relaxation, we discussed muscle-to-mind and mind-to-muscle techniques. The present chapter stays with the concept of mind-to-muscle but discusses a cognitive technique that will help you to perceive your state of arousal in a positive, productive manner. In order to do this, you can use two techniques: self-talk, *your internal 'voice'* and cognitive restructuring, ***changing your thought patterns***. Self-talk and cognitive restructuring can be thought of as two sides to the same coin: self-talk can only be successful if the thoughts in a teacher's head are positive. If those thoughts are negative, they can be changed, or restructured to become positive. This, in essence, is what cognitive restructuring aims to do. The following examples will highlight this point.

## Chapter objectives

- Understand how self-talk can assist you in a variety of situations.
- Consider personal and specific self-talk expressions for a variety of occasions.
- Understand how to retrain your thoughts through cognitive restructuring.

## What is self-talk?

Self-talk is the mental activity that occurs whenever an individual thinks and makes perceptions and beliefs conscious. ***It is talking in the mind, rather than aloud***. Self-talk helps you to stay focused on strategic elements of your teaching. In practice, you might use the word, 'Focus' to signify the exact moment you feel your concentration slipping when engaged with your planning, preparation or assessment. It is the equivalent of hitting the 'turbo mode', narrowing your focus, providing a shot of energy and leading to successfully completing the task at hand.

## When should self-talk be used?

Different types of self-talk exist, for different situations: correcting bad habits, refocusing, building self-confidence, controlling effort and modifying arousal levels. You need to be aware of each of these to help you understand how the technique will be of use to you.

### Correcting bad habits
This is rather like self-coaching or self-instruction. Here, self-talk is used to question how you are presenting yourself in the classroom, your confidence, scanning the class for students who may be experiencing difficulties, the pace and progress of your lesson, and so on. Self-talk may be used to make corrections when you are learning a new skill and need to develop and refine it, for example, using a new software package, or for checking your understanding of a concept you are to teach.

## Activity 10.1

Consider one aspect of your practice that you know you could improve on. This could be 'talk to a point on the back wall so everyone can hear', or 'ensure I leave plenty of time for the plenary'. Make a note of this in your journal.

## Refocusing

Cue words and statements such as 'be here', 'here and now' and any others you feel comfortable with are useful for bringing you back to the reality of now.

You might have lyrics from favourite songs that may help you here, or you may want to find inspirational lyrics through a search website (for example, www.songlyrics.com). For instance, a line in Toni Braxton's song 'Let It Flow' has the lyrics, 'Just let go ... And let it flow ... Everything's gonna work out right'. From this the lyrics 'Just let go ... And let it flow' could mean to stop struggling against something, relax, let what happens happen – good advice if you're worrying over something! Another is, 'While everyone's lost, the battle is won ... With all these things that I've done' by The Killers. Be careful in your selection. 'Help!' by the Beatles would not go down too nicely!

 ## Activity 10.2

Select a phrase that will keep you focused on the present, something to bring your attention back if it starts to wander.

Secondly, consider a song that helps to motivate or stimulate you in some way. You may even want to make your own playlist of such motivational songs.

## Building self-confidence

Self-confidence is a vital element of successful performance. Teachers who lack self-confidence are immediately disadvantaged and face an uphill battle. If you are lacking in self-confidence, you may enhance it, indirectly through self-talk. Self-confidence was discussed in greater depth in Chapter 4.

## Controlling effort

Having focused on the task in hand, it is important that teachers *'stay in tune'*. Self-talk can be used to keep the level of effort high, avoiding any lapses in performance and concentration. Indeed, the phrases 'stay in tune' or 'stay on the pace' are good examples that help to control effort levels (although feel free to take ownership over your own similar phrase). As a safety net, refocusing should be used if effort does falter too much. A problem may occur, however, when somebody else tells you to put in more effort as this can make you frustrated if you are already committing 100 per cent. Such requests are irritating! A good self-talk response would be something like, 'I will put in the effort that feels right for me.'

 **Activity 10.3**

As with Activity 10.1, consider a personal phrase that helps you to maintain your effort should it start to flag.

## Modifying arousal levels

Self-talk can be used to psyche yourself up or calm yourself down. Essentially it is used to control your arousal level depending on how nervous you are and whether the level of arousal is facilitative or debilitative. This also depends on how you perceive that excitement or arousal and is linked to your changes in mood. If you do not feel in the right frame of mind to teach, you can use self-talk to alter your present mood state. Find out what the problem is through accurately defining the problem, seek the solution, and then use self-talk to confirm that you are moving towards that solution.

Every action begins with a thought. Consequently, if you think positively then you will get used to acting positively. You might start by telling yourself that *'I believe I can do it'* and that you have been practising it, with some success, in teaching. Then you can continue with *'you know you can do it'*, backed up with the knowledge of the training and preparation you have invested.

Eventually your confidence will increase as well. Sometimes, others may mistake this confidence for arrogance, but this could merely be extreme confidence overflowing into speech. In the teaching world, teachers who use positive self-talk, persist in their quality and commitment to their work. Consequently, self-talk has the additional bonus of helping to retain or increase motivation when the going gets tougher than normal.

## How should self-talk be used?

By its very nature of being an internal voice, self-talk cannot be measured directly. We must ensure, however, that you understand how to use self-talk and how to measure progress if it is used. It is also important to explain that negative thoughts may lead to your experiencing a mental block, which could have a detrimental effect on performance.

Although the methods outlined below are subjective, a check can be made at opportune moments to establish whether or not they are working adequately. We will outline three methods for using self-talk in teaching. You should decide which works best for you, or whether a combination of methods provides a useful variation on the theme.

## Retrospection

Think back to very good and not so good performances. Try to recall your pre- and post-thoughts and feelings. It is important to remember, however, that using recall methods can lead to distorted and inaccurate incidents. Psychologists know from research that our memory is not always as accurate as we think it is. *If you start to keep a log or journal, you can use this information in the future when you need to 'look back'.* If we ask you to recall events from a particular event three years ago, you may struggle. If you kept records, you can give us all the information we need.

## Imagery

Re-create performances or sequences mentally, as we will discuss in Chapter 11. Once again it is necessary to recall and record thoughts and feelings associated with the performance, using these to remember the positive self-talk before and after the event.

## Self-talk logs

Keep daily records of any self-talk that you have carried out and make a note of what the situation was when you carried out that self-talk. This also helps you to assess whether you are predominantly positive or negative in your self-talk.

*It is essential that you identify patterns of self-talk before you can develop the technique for personal use.* Several methods exist for you to use, including: thought stopping, visual cues and physical signals.

## Thought stopping

It is possible to use a thought or cue to interrupt those unwanted thoughts as they occur. You can quickly say out loud *'stop'* as soon as you know you are saying or thinking an undesirable thought. It is important that you consider the thought, if there is time. Evaluate and reflect on it, but then you need to insert another, more positive thought in its place.

### Visual cues

You can use a visual cue, such as a mental picture of a **red traffic light**, representing 'stop'. Again, you will need quickly to insert another more positive thought in its place and then change the red traffic light to green.

### Physical signals

You can use physical movements, such as **snapping your fingers** to represent 'stop'. Yet again, you need quickly to insert another more positive thought in its place.

---

 ## Activity 10.4

The task below will help you to identify where self-talk may help you. Follow the instructions below, decide how many of them are in your control and work on putting positive self-talk statements in place to overcome any challenges you have identified.

**Instruction**

1 Recall some aspect of your teaching experience in which you felt you could have produced a more successful performance. This could be working with students, or planning, preparation and assessment time.

2 Write down what you did, what you felt and what you said. Look critically at your narrative for negative thoughts. How could you change some of the negative thoughts? Are there some areas where you are thinking positively? Try not to punish yourself for these, give yourself some credit!

3 List ten of your most common thoughts when you engaged with teaching.

4 Look at the list you have produced. Have you focused on issues outside of your control? Have you been unduly negative?

5 For every thought write a positive statement or a self-focused alternative.

6 All you need to do now is to recognize when this occurs and insert the new positive thought in its place!

---

## Self-talk should become automatic or second nature

As we pointed out in Chapter 2, if a teacher thinks too much about what they are doing, these very thought processes may distract him or her from the task, by disrupting the automatic performance. However, self-talk is about 'key words' or phrases. *It is mentally economical and it feeds into teaching.* As soon as you begin to focus too much on exactly the task at hand, concentrating too much on one element, your attention will be diverted and you will begin to make mistakes. You should be aiming to be able to use self-talk automatically rather than having to think too much about it. In order to do this, you have to go through the process of thinking too much about it. An example of this is midway through a lesson and you get caught up thinking about the next lesson. Automatically a bellowing voice comes from inside, 'Focus!' In a single word, you have given yourself the guidance on monitoring the class, monitoring the development of the lesson, being clear and calm and not getting distracted from an incident that may be escalating. This takes practice … Take the challenge!

## Cognitive restructuring: how to get the most from your inner voice

Arguably, none of us 'see' the world as it really is. Instead, we perceive the world. We see it as we think it exists for us. It is all a matter of perspective! Think about each student in your class – they have a different view of the room, the board, you. Our perspective is shaped by the way we think, our attitudes, beliefs, superstitions, stereotypes, and so on. Cognitive restructuring is derived from a psychotherapy technique developed back in the 1960s by Ellis (1962). Basically, *it aims to direct us towards modifying self-defeating, irrational and anxiety-provoking cognitions or thoughts*. It can be used to restructure these thoughts and to alter irrational or 'bad' thoughts. It is relatively easy to spot negative thoughts and substitute them with positive thoughts before they get too serious. With practice, you will stop negative thoughts before they emerge. There should be nothing negative in your head when you are teaching, regardless of what is happening.

Instead, you will have plenty of things to keep your focus. A combination of cognitive restructuring with self-talk can be used to provide self-reward and to increase your effort.

## When should you use cognitive restructuring?

Cognitive restructuring can be used in various situations. For example, it is effective in reducing anxiety and increasing levels of coping under adverse conditions. It is also useful in increasing self-confidence, as well as the motivation for teaching. If you have trouble with making a start on your marking, then perhaps cognitive restructuring can help you to think differently about how you approach it.

## Stages in developing cognitive restructuring

Cognitive restructuring is not as difficult as it may initially appear. It typically comprises four stages. You need to be aware that your beliefs, perceptions and assumptions influence emotional arousal. Consider the perceptions of a day-to-day occurrence, yours and your line manager/head. If they have just asked you to complete an additional task, you may feel frustration. You should identify underlying thoughts to recognize any potential irrational, self-defeating foundations you may have, such as 'I am always given extra responsibilities, they must not like me' or 'when will I have time to do this?' *Once you have identified these irrational thoughts, you need actively to criticize them (your thoughts, NOT your line manager/head!), replacing them with thoughts that prevent or reduce maladaptive anxiety.* For example, in the situation of being given extra responsibility, you could replace the thoughts with 'they must think I do a good job and can handle the extra responsibility'. *Finally, you should practise and rehearse new thoughts, applying them to relevant situations.*

 Activity 10.5

You might like to use the following four questions to guide you in deciding whether the thoughts are irrational or distorted. We use these questions, based on psychology literature, because they are practical and elicit almost immediate responses from teachers.

Are the beliefs based on objective reality?
Do the thoughts help you reach your short- and long-term goals?
Are the thoughts helpful or self-destructive?
Do the thoughts reduce emotional conflict with yourself or others?

Having established that some thoughts may be irrational or distorted, you should list them on a sheet of paper, in no specific order. The table below provides some examples of irrational thoughts. We have labelled the column 'self-defeating thoughts', in order to use the phrase, 'self-enhancing thought' for the cognitively restructured thought. You may identify with them, or you may be able to list your own examples.

| Self-defeating thought | Self-enhancing thought |
| --- | --- |
| I have the term's planning to complete. | Planning takes time but if done properly now, it will make the term easier. |
| That was stupid of me! | Ease off. Everyone makes mistakes. |

| Self-defeating thought | Self-enhancing thought |
|---|---|
|  | Shrug it off and put your mind on what you want to do. |
| I have no time to do this! | I can arrange my time more efficiently to ensure I can fulfil all my tasks. |
| I can't concentrate. | I will go for a walk or get some exercise, then I will be invigorated to get back on with the task. |
| I don't want to do x or y. | I have many things to focus on. If I do this first, I will be able to look forward to the things I enjoy. |

Once you have listed any negative thoughts that you may have before, during or after a day in the classroom, it then becomes relatively straightforward to use the examples of self-enhancing thoughts listed above to restructure any negative thoughts that have been identified.

*It is imperative that you believe these new thoughts. Anything less than total belief will be met with failure.* We would also ask you to identify 'key' words or phrases that will help you to keep focused and motivated during your teaching. These might include: 'come on!', 'yes!', 'that was good', 'I can do it', 'smooth!', 'calm' … as opposed to 'oh, sh*t!' or 'breathe'.

This section has provided examples of self-enhancing thoughts that you may use during sessions to fend off self-defeating thoughts before they happen. If any creep in, you must address them rationally in relation to other things that are working positively. Your anxiety levels should remain 'comfortable'. In the next chapter, we will discuss how to use mental imagery to improve your teaching.

## One-minute summary

Talking to yourself is a quick and easy psychological strategy to address a number of issues, such as correcting bad habits, refocusing, developing self-confidence, controlling effort and modifying your arousal levels. Although self-talk is verbally orientated, albeit in your mind, you could similarly use visual signs (like a traffic light) or kinaesthetic actions (like clicking your fingers) to elicit a response.

It is important to ensure that in utilizing self-talk, you adhere to the positive. Rather than saying 'Don't do this' rephrase it as 'I will do this'. Remember we use positive behavioural strategies for our students, so why not with ourselves!

## Short-term strategies for the here and now

- Find out which visual cue works for you. Is it the mental *stop* sign, the red traffic light, or is it auditory … a very loud mental 'STOPPPP!'
- Practise stopping a negative thought every time it comes into your head (it doesn't have to be confined to school-based thoughts).

  - o Next, practise inserting a 'new', positive thought in its place after the *stop* cue.
  - o Once you are able to control this (thus showing that you can use the technique), move on to school-specific negatives.

- Consider a phrase to focus your attention, for example, 'I am focused on the here and now'.
- Consider a phrase to maintain your effort, for example, 'I will complete my marking by 4 p.m.'.

  Or,

- 'I don't care what you say about my time-keeping, because I know that I was in at 7.30 a.m., have been productive, and I am leaving at 4.30 p.m. to balance things out.'
- If you find yourself in a situation where you feel your confidence diminishing, say to yourself one of the following phrases at least five times in a row:

  - o 'I am a calm and confident teacher.'
  - o 'Every time I take a deep breath, I will be more relaxed.'

- How do you feel?

## Mentoring issues

As with some of the other areas raised in this book, your mentor may not be aware of the use of self-talk. Even if they do use it, our experience suggests that most people use it in a negative way, that is, starting with 'Don't … '. (You will be familiar with this, for example, 'beating yourself up' when struggling with something.)

You may be able to consider how you can use self-talk to achieve one of your goals or targets that have been set, so discussing this with your mentor may enable you to consider the most relevant phrases to use.

## 📖 Further reading

Hamilton, R.A., Scott, D. and Macdougall, M.P. (2007) 'Assessing the effectiveness of self-talk interventions on endurance performance', *Journal of Applied Sport Psychology*, 19: 226–39.
This paper explores different types of self-talk on endurance (in this case cycling), but contains relevant, transferable information. Don't be put off by the 'academic nature' of the paper. Take what you need from the introduction and discussion.

Hay, L.L. (2004) *I Can Do It: How to Use Affirmations to Change Your Life*. Carlsbad, CA: Hay House.
This short book also contains a CD which work together in order to understand and develop your own affirmations.

Helmstetter, S. (1991) *What to Say When You Talk to Your Self*. London: Thorsons.
The book is quite dated although is a 'classic' in terms of using positive self-talk.

McWilliams, J.-R. and McWilliams, P. (2001) *You Can't Afford the Luxury of a Negative Thought: A Guide to Positive Thinking*. London: Thorsons.
Another book which is practical in nature and effectively structured in turning negative thoughts to positive thoughts.

# 11

# Is Hallucinating the Second Sign of 'Madness'? Mental Imagery

## Introduction

Visualization is seeing a picture of an event in your mind. Mental imagery takes this picture and converts it into a sequence similar to mentally playing a DVD. At a simple level, visualization may involve the storage of a single picture or basic moving image, for example, of a classroom. In contrast, mental imagery is an active, dynamic process, in which the 'image' is continuously modified as if it were an enhanced video recording. You may already use this technique. Many teachers believe that they 'know' the classroom in their minds. The question you should ask yourself is, 'Are you able to *see* a *picture* or a *moving sequence*?' You may have a visual image of the classroom, but there is so much more that you could include to 'make it real'.

As we demonstrated with imagery-related relaxation in Chapter 9, other senses may be included to enhance the quality of the internal 'experience'.

You may adopt one of two perspectives: internal or external. It is important to discover whether you adopt a perspective where you experience imagery from the point of view of being seen in the image or, whether you experience from within, 'looking' outwards as it were.

In practical terms, the common consensus in the literature is that teachers may benefit from employing imagery techniques. Although the exact mechanism remains speculative, the mere perception of 'having been there before in your head' seems to pay dividends when you present in the physical reality.

## Chapter objectives

- Understand the difference between visualization and imagery.
- Appreciate how imagery works and how it can help you professionally.
- Recognize the differences between internal and external imagery.
- Develop effective imagery skills for a specific purpose.
- Plan and write your own imagery script.

## What is visualization?

The clue to answering this question is evident in the root of the word: visual. Visualization suggests that a picture is stored, for example, the classroom. This 'picture' is an internal copy of a photograph or image on a computer screen. While it may be useful to evoke memories that accompany the image, it is far from 'real'. A more complex version of visualization may be of the same location but played as a video, again only using the visual sense. Although this is arguably closer to reality than the photograph-based equivalent, it still lacks the complexity necessary for a 'lifelike' representation of it to be stored in the human brain.

As we have said elsewhere, humans are visually dominant. If you take the time to reflect on how important sight is to your own daily life and, indeed your passion for teaching, you can understand why there is such a heavy reliance on the visual sense. Nevertheless, this leaves a wealth of untapped information provided by other sensory systems that can be incorporated into visualization to provide a higher-quality experience. This is where mental imagery goes a step further.

## What is mental imagery?

Robert Weinberg and Daniel Gould suggest that, 'Imagery is actually a form of simulation ... similar to a real sensory experience (e.g., seeing, feeling or hearing), but the entire experience occurs in the mind' (2007: 296). You may not realize, but you may readily identify with this. Consider the occasions when your start to a lesson may not have been as smooth as you would have liked. The class take time to settle and prepare and from the outset you seem to not have their full attention. At the end of the lesson you may retire to the staffroom running over in your mind how you could have started the lesson differently to bring a calm, orderly, focused start to the lesson.

The idea that other senses can be incorporated into mental imagery is not surprising. The human brain comprises many systems and sub-systems, all of which communicate in some way with each other, whether this is directly or indirectly. Indeed, if you look out of the window at this very moment and see a vehicle go past, you will more than likely also hear that vehicle. The brain does not store these pieces of information as two separate perceptions. Rather, they are combined. Why not therefore, use the senses to your advantage when creating a mental image? *The more detail you can add, the more realistic the experience.*

When we talk of mental imagery, we are concerned with so much more than just the visual system. In order to avoid any misleading or confusing subtleties in terminology, we would favour the term 'mental rehearsal' to encompass all aspects of acquiring, developing and refining a mental representation of a forthcoming lesson.

## How does imagery work?

The exact mechanism behind imagery remains elusive. Nevertheless, imagery seems to convince your brain that imagining a situation is syn-onymous with reality. This is conveniently illustrated through dreaming. For example, you may have had the fairly common, 'I'm late' dream. You have an important event/appointment/lesson observation tomor-row and you suddenly wake up in a cold sweat during the night, because you have been dreaming about missing the alarm clock, getting up late, vehicle won't start, stuck in traffic and not getting there on time. This, of course, is all taking place in your subconscious mind. Nevertheless, it is sufficiently 'real' to elicit physiological changes in your autonomic nervous system, such that you wake in a panic. Essentially therefore, *the events in your mind are 'real'* until your conscious mind wakes and evaluates the reality of the situation, that is, it is in fact 2.00 a.m. and you have plenty of time.

Psychologists are not entirely certain exactly how imagery works and many theories exist. However, for our purposes, we can take selected elements of each theory and apply it for practical purposes to teaching.

## Psycho-neuro-muscular patterns

Stored 'psycho-neuro-muscular' patterns are thought to be identical to those patterns that exist in response to actual events. This means that the way in which you think helps your brain to access the correct muscular pattern that is needed. So, *the more you practise the action mentally, the stronger the connection and the quicker you will access it when needed*.

Imagery can also lead to an increase in electrical activity in the muscles associated with the task. If electromyography (EMG) electrodes (which record muscle activation) were attached to your arms or legs and we asked you sit still but to run through making a cup of coffee, we would be able to record some muscular activity in the relevant muscles (that are *not* actually moving). Mental rehearsal of this kind is akin to using a route map to discover how to get to a destination and then to practise it mentally until it becomes second nature.

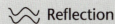 Reflection

Consider the physical actions relevant to your role: depending on the subject you teach or are planning to teach, there may be a different focus. For example, it could be demonstrating a passing skill in physical education, or the stages you need to go through on the board to start a certain programme.

## Symbolic learning

It may be that thoughts/cognition rather than electrical activity in the muscles is responsible. A 'blueprint' is formed, highlighting all possible solutions to a response. *You simply need to select the correct solution from the blueprint and execute the response*. A cognitively based task, involving strategy, such as assertively responding to an escalating incident in the classroom, would be best suited to the symbolic learning theory.

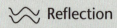 Reflection

Consider different ways of responding to a student interrupting the lesson.

## Bio-information

Bio-information is the storage of two types of information in the brain: stimulus characteristics and response characteristics. This is similar to computer programs that work on an 'If X happens, then do Y' principle. Response characteristics are said to describe **how you respond to the stimuli in the given situation**. Physiological responses are particularly important here. Bio-informational theory holds that you need to incorporate both types of characteristics into your imagery so that you can develop, amend and strengthen them.

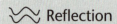 Reflection

Consider a student putting their hand up to get your attention. Do you call across the classroom to ask them how you can help, or do you walk over to the student?

## Attention-arousal setting

Attention-arousal setting refers to how imagery can be used to increase attention, improve concentration, heighten focus, and mentally prepare for the day ahead. **It is about accessing all available sensory information, combining it and using it to focus your attention and arousal level** for your teaching.

In putting these elements together, for example, you might imagine your heart rate increasing as the lesson gets ever closer. You might 'feel' some tension in your body as you enter into the classroom. You might 'feel' clammy hands before the class comes in. You might incorporate the sounds of the students entering and how the noise makes you feel. Does it increase anxiety or does it provide confidence? Similarly, how do you feel about your elevated heart rate? Does it make you feel anxious and tense, or does it give you a feeling of supreme energy and power to do the job in hand? Psychologically speaking, if you incorporate positive elements into your imagery, these will inspire confidence in your ability to succeed. In refining the imagery, you should expect to 'lose' the tension, clamminess and adjust your elevated heart rate to an optimal level. In short, you are completely ready for teaching.

It is worth noting at this point that the vital element of bio-informational theory is that the imagery resulting from your development of stimulus and response (or antecedent and consequence) characteristics is specific to you: it is a mental 'fingerprint', unique to you and based on the cognitive meaning you assign to the characteristics.

For example, the concentration and attentional focus required to execute a successful start to a lesson is arguably very different from that required for the full lesson. Mental imagery should be different for and specific to each situation. You need to be able to distinguish the differences between each situation. This will enable you to develop a suitable 'imagery sequence' for each one, which you will then be able to practise so that you can execute the appropriate reaction when you are teaching.

One headteacher reported to us that they were concerned that a student always seemed to be sleeping in the staffroom during break. Her concern was that the student was either working too hard, or partying too much! Knowing the student had recently attended one of our seminars on mental imagery, we responded that although it may appear they were 'nodding off', they were actually using mental imagery to focus their mind and concentrate on the coming lesson before going back into the classroom. This 'setting' of the mind would seem to be similar to flicking the 'I am ready' switch, which puts you into 'optimal performance mode'.

It seems therefore, that several pieces of the jigsaw exist and you need to consider exactly how you might prepare for a successful performance in the classroom. We shall discuss some of these jigsaw pieces as the chapter progresses.

## Operationalizing imagery

In practical terms, it is possible to use mental imagery in three different, yet complementary ways:

- Learning and developing physical skills. The physical elements of any skill can be rehearsed mentally if the necessary information is available.
- Developing psychological skills, such as reducing anxiety or 'psyching up'. This ought to be useful in situations where you need to deal with pressure.
- Developing and refining perceptual skills, such as monitoring the class for understanding and engagement with the lesson.

 Activity 11.1

In your journal, write down an example where imagery could be used for each of the following:

- Learning and developing physical skills.
- Developing psychological skills.
- Developing and refining perceptual skills.

## Which perspective: internal or external imagery?

It is widely regarded that 'performers' such as teachers either create imagery where they see themselves in the situation (an external perspective) or they see the situation as if it were from their own eyes (an internal perspective). A working example using the classroom highlights these differences.

*If you adopt an external perspective*, you might take a perspective looking through the classroom window into the room, where you see the students sitting at their desks, together with displays and resources.

You see the teacher's desk, the board and someone standing at the front of the room. You see the person speaking, turning to the board, then back to the students. You see the person work confidently, moving around the class as required. Of course, the person you are looking at is yourself. This perspective may not be as beneficial as the internal perspective, which we will discuss next. Nevertheless, if you are lacking in confidence, this perspective will do you no harm whatsoever.

*If you adopt an internal perspective*, you will take a perspective from behind your own eyes, looking out of and around the classroom, where you see the students, the board, the resources, and so on.

You monitor the class and bring the students to attention, you turn to the board and highlight the lesson objectives, you move around the room confidently monitoring students' engagement. We could spend the next few pages enhancing this explanation, but we are sure that the message is now clear.

The decision regarding which perspective you should adopt would inevitably depend upon the underlying reasons for using imagery. For example, if you need to rehearse your routine mentally, in order to familiarize yourself with the lesson, reduce potential stressors and suchlike, then it may be preferable to adopt an internal perspective. If, on the other hand, you need to boost self-confidence, then adopting an external perspective would enable you to 'see' yourself performing successfully in the situation. As a result, this may do a lot to maintain, or indeed boost, self-confidence in advance of the actual lesson.

If anything, external imagery is arguably more difficult to achieve successfully than internal imagery. It is, however, vital that you practise each perspective. It is dangerous to assume that you already possess sufficient imagery skills, even if you believe that you use imagery. You should carry out an 'audit' of your imagery. *Do you use all senses?* If not why not? If you do, then are you including the level of detail covered in this chapter? You should then develop and refine them before practising using the 'correct tool for the job'. For example, we would not advocate using external imagery if a teacher's self-confidence is high as this may lead to psychological conflicts with motivational issues, which we discuss in Chapter 3.

**Activity 11.2**

In your journal note down the differences between internal and external imagery.

Consider which of these you would find easier to work with. Why is this?

## Using all of the senses to enhance imagery

As mentioned above, humans are a visually dominant species. As a result, one might argue that we have become rather complacent. If the information you receive from your visual system is sufficient for you to 'do the job', then why use valuable time and energy in acquiring information from other senses? Of course, this is not strictly the case. ***The human brain constantly receives information from all sensory systems.*** However, it does not necessarily process all of the incoming information at the same level or in the same depth. Nevertheless it is possible, with practice, to train the brain in processing information that is relevant to the task in hand. In short, the more usable information one has, the easier, and indeed more appropriate, the decision becomes. The only time that this situation becomes detrimental is when the information is meaningless and, if this happens, an inappropriate choice of decision is made.

So what information might the other senses provide? The next time you are in the classroom, start to become aware of what your senses are telling you. What can you see? You should be able to see the students, the classroom, how they act with one another, with the subject content, with the teacher, all contextually relevant pieces of information. What can you hear? You may be able to hear students talking about a task, whether the talk is constructive to the outcome, you may hear noise from other classes, perhaps you can hear noise from the playground or sports field, and so on. What can you feel physically? You may feel the texture of the floor as you walk around the classroom from the carpeted area to the wooden/tiled areas. What is the temperature – too hot or cold? What can you smell? (See Activity 11.3.) The gustatory, or taste, sense plays little if any role in providing information in a teaching environment (unless it is food technology, or there is a new brand of coffee you are using to fuel your body – see Chapter 5 on nutrition). However, you might notice the 'dry mouth' sensation that some teachers get before a lesson. A dry mouth is quite natural and is part of the human body's defence mechanism; 'fight or flight', a readiness to do, or react to a situation. As you read this, you may identify with any, most or all of these examples. If they have happened in reality, then why not incorporate them into mental imagery? In doing so, ***you will be providing yourself*** *with mental imagery as lifelike as the real thing, but in your head. You can rehearse this imagery until it becomes second nature and, if the underlying theory holds true, you will be strengthening the connections within your brain so that you can select the right choice at the right time and be completely familiar with it.*

 Activity 11.3

Go into your classroom, close your eyes ... and sniff! Be aware of the smells in your classroom at different points of the day.

Example:

　8.30 a.m. – Coffee! – Staffroom
　11.30 a.m. – 'Body odour' – School Hall or gym after PE
　12.00 p.m. – Lunchtime smells
　1.00 p.m. – Damp coats hanging up if it has been raining
　2.30 p.m. – Chlorine – Swimming baths for lesson
　4 p.m. – Disinfectant

(Of course the examples used are dependent on the age range you work with. The science corridor in a secondary school, bonfire smoke if you have been working with 'Forest Schools', and so on.)

Look at this list. Can you re-create these in the privacy of your own home? This might involve bringing physical resources with you. For example, sit at home, sharpen a pencil and put it up to your nose to smell it. Close your eyes and think of the classroom. You should now mentally be in the classroom. The smell has acted as a cue to fool your brain into thinking that you are actually there.

Any time you want to mentally rehearse a classroom-based or other learning activity, think about whether you can use an odour to re-create the activity.

Please note that the olfactory sense (the sense of smell) is an extremely powerful sense that links us almost immediately to memories and emotions (Castle, Van Toller and Milligan, 2000). Look out for a new book on the sense of smell, by the eminent olfactory psychologist, Professor Steve Van Toller, entitled *The Nose and I*, due to be published in 2009.

As this section highlights, if a teacher incorporates information provided by various senses into their mental imagery, the imagery should be vivid and of high quality. This is hardly surprising, given that although the human brain comprises many systems, it is also a part of a system. Consequently, the brain processes information from a variety of interdependent 'sub-systems', such as the senses, the endocrine system (responsible for hormone release), cardiovascular system (responsible for fluctuations in heart rate) and autonomic nervous system (responsible for the 'stress' response), to name but a few. This interdependence also operates for psychological skills techniques. For example, combining mental imagery with relaxation can be extremely powerful.

## Effective use of mental imagery skills

At least three key issues emerge if mental imagery is to be used effectively in preparation for teaching: belief, lucidity or vividness, and control.

### Belief

At an early point in proceedings it is vital to recognize that mental imagery will only aid preparation for an event if you believe in it. Let's face it, if we ask you to do something that you don't believe you can do, it is unlikely to work at all. If we can show you by helping you to obtain your own examples of it working, then you are more likely to accept the technique and gain benefits from its use.

### Lucidity or vividness

We have already discussed the importance of acquiring information from many sources, for incorporation into mental imagery. A lucid piece of mental imagery contains high-quality, detailed, information of varying levels of significance. It is as close to the 'real thing' as one can be but is in the mind.

Consider how successful computer games have become since technology has enabled programmers to re-create so-called reality within the game. You would have to admit that you could get so 'involved' in the game that your brain is deceived into believing that you are actually part of it. Although there are no 'classroom-environment' computer games (and let's face, why would there be!), mental imagery is the equivalent of the most realistic computer game, but you can make mental imagery even better, because it is specific to your own needs. Think in terms of mentally writing your own, bespoke, computer game for your own classroom. Of course, why not extend this principle; teach your students how to use imagery and then ask them to write imagery sequences to suit the learning objectives of your lesson (we would be keen to receive communication on this from you).

## Control

Control is a vital, yet sometimes overlooked aspect of mental imagery. If you have practised your pace and timing in lessons but you always seem to have left no time for clearing up, there is a danger that you may incorporate this error into the mental imagery. Consequently, you will overrun every time you practise mentally and every time you practise for real. *It is imperative that you are able to control the imagery to your advantage.* It will help you to image the outcome that you want, rather than the events leading to a lesser outcome. Psychologists widely agree that stressful situations are made worse when there is no element of control and this may lead to a phenomenon known as 'learned helplessness' (Seligman, 1975). In short, if you always overrun in practise, you simply accept that it will happen time and time again. We would argue that it is possible, through controlling your mental imagery, to achieve the desired outcome. For example, you are more likely to complete the lesson if you imagine everything cleared, with the class sitting ready to go, perhaps using some quick-fire questions on the concepts just covered to take you to the bell. As a teacher, your desire never to give up is evident all the time. Do not lose sight of this when you are in the situation described above. We have discussed having a 'bank' of mental imagery for 'what if' situations. This could be one of them. So, if you feel your pace is wrong part way through the lesson, how will it feel, how will you control your imagery, and yourself so that you rehearse getting yourself out of the situation. In effect, you are rehearsing 'worst case scenarios' and, if they happen in reality, you are practised in dealing with them.

Control of imagery is possibly the hardest thing to master and it takes practice. Do not be disheartened if you need to spend a little longer than expected on this aspect of the technique. It will, however, pay dividends in the long run. Of course, it is very easy to sit here, on a cold winter's morning, providing advice on how to plan for teaching. However, as you are probably more than aware with teaching, nothing is ever as clear-cut as this. Nevertheless, it now becomes possible to develop a set of different imagery scenarios for different 'what if' situations.

Having discussed the theory behind mental imagery, it is necessary at this point in the chapter, to move on to practicalities of developing and practising mental imagery. The starting point for this is by thinking about and writing an imagery script.

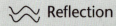 Reflection

If you were to develop a computer game which simulated teaching, how would you make it:

- Believable?
- As realistic as possible?
- How much control would the 'player' have? How do they operate in the 'game'?

## Writing an imagery script

Before beginning to help you to write an imagery script, it is important to establish how successfully you can create a mental image at the moment. You should respond to the following statements and then revisit them after you have developed your imagery technique. You will then be able to assess your progress.

### Activity 11.4

Tick the box on the right if your answer to each statement is 'yes'. The more boxes you are able to tick, the more successful you are at mental imagery. Remember to be honest!!

I can see myself in the classroom

I can feel the classroom atmosphere

I can see the students actively learning

I can feel myself getting 'psyched up' for the lesson

I can make up new teaching responses and strategies in my head

I can see myself successfully following my lesson plan

I can imagine myself being in control in difficult situations

I can see myself successfully overcoming challenging situations

I can see myself giving 100 per cent during the lesson

I can imagine myself appearing self-confident in front of the class

I can hear the sounds of the classroom

I can hear the sounds outside of the classroom

I can smell the odour of the classroom

I can smell the odour outside of the classroom

Use this chapter to help you develop your imagery for any boxes left unticked. You may also use the chapter to help in enhancing the vividness and clarity of your mental imagery. In doing so, you will be re-creating and practising these situations in your mind, remaining calm, focused and in control of your thoughts/feelings.

Having established your existing level of imagery ability, this information can be used to help develop an imagery script. It would be unwise, however, to launch straight into writing the imagery script before we have given you an idea of what is and is not important in the environment. To do this, we would like you to start by taking a mental journey around your living room at home.

Try to picture the shape of the room, the location of furniture, television, fireplace, tables, and so on. Then picture the colour of the walls, the location of mirrors, prints or photographs. Picture the location of any windows or doors and the view through these. A basic representation of your living room should now be emerging in your mind. When you are happy that you can picture the scene, it is necessary to add increasing levels of detail. Picture the colour of the carpet or floor covering. Has the sun faded it in patches? Are there any stains on it and is it frayed anywhere? If you are unable to answer these questions, have a look the next time you are in the living room, check them and incorporate the new information into the image. You can also add the colour of the walls, damaged areas, position of light switches and perhaps radiators. Next might be the visual texture of the walls and whether the prints or photographs are hanging straight or skewed. ***Your mental image is now beginning to build to a high degree of complexity.*** If you build the picture in this way, it becomes possible to take this to the finest level of detail. The point is to show you how powerful the technique can be as you pick up more and more information from the environment. We tend to concentrate only on the visual system for the 'living room' example and pay less attention to other senses.

Now you are ready to move on to mental imagery for the classroom, we can include your other senses. An example might include asking you to 'feel' how comfortable your seat is at your desk when marking. How does the pen feel in your hand? How far can you reach up the board to write something? What does it feel like to walk around the classroom – is there easy access?

Now think about a lesson you have taught previously, one you are happy with and know very well. Start to build up a mental imagery sequence of the lesson. The example provided below highlights this.

---

The class is lining up outside in the playground. I am already there ready to bring them to order and ensure they walk in an orderly way into the class.

I tell the students exactly what I want them to do when they go into the class. After removing their coats, they need to sit quietly at their desks with their individual white boards.

I tell the students to write down five mathematic questions to give to the person sitting next to them.

---

I monitor the students as they come into the room, ensuring everyone is doing as requested, reminding them they need their boards.

All the students are writing down their questions and calmly passing their boards to one another, then they are answering the questions.

I set the timer on the board for two minutes then monitor the students to keep them on task.

The two minutes pass and I tell the students to return their boards so their partner can check their answers. I set the timer for another two minutes.

I give the students one minute to feed back to their partner on how they did and any mistakes.

Once the time has expired, I ask the class to focus on the board again, where the lesson objectives are displayed.

I ask them to check their understanding of the words in order to ensure they focus on the key concepts of the lesson.

If you are familiar with starting a lesson as in the example script above, we would like to think that you are able to picture each element as it relates to the class you work with (you may not actually teach mathematics, so feel free to adapt). Of course, not all of the information you need will be in the script. For example, the script above takes place at the start of a new year and students may not be used to the routine which is being established. Is it the first or last lesson of the day? How will this affect the students? The weather conditions may affect the students: it may be a very hot summer's day or cold and wet. If, for example it is a very hot summer's day, think about what the widely renowned 'super-teacher' Phil Beadle would do (see www.philbeadle.com).

Having produced a script of the kind shown above it should be used to get a grasp for the intricacies of the lesson and become imprinted on your mind. You can then reduce it to something more practical to remind yourself of the stages, for example:

Be outside as they line up
Sit at desks, white boards out.
Five questions then swap.
Two minutes on timer.
Hand board back. Mark partner's work.
Feedback to partner.
Lesson objectives.
Check understanding.

You can see how this script has been created from the previous one. It is not the words that make the script. Rather it is the visual imagery in your mind that brings the script to life. If these words don't allow you to 'see' the lesson, then you need to adapt them until the lesson is brought to life. Keep practising until it appears for you!

*A correctly designed mental imagery sequence can be used to rehearse even the finest of detail, to the point where it becomes second nature.* As pointed out earlier, this should free up available mental resources for strategy. Table 11.1 can be used as a template for writing an imagery script. It contains details that act as a mental rehearsal for the events leading up to the start of the lesson outlined above. See if you can identify with it. The script can easily be adapted to suit any lesson for any subject.

 **Activity 11.5**

Reviewing the last section of this chapter, specifically Table 11.1 (below), consider developing your own imagery script. A downloadable form is available on the website.

**Table 11.1**  Example mental imagery script

| Phase 1: Basic awareness | Phase 2: Inclusion of details | | Phase 3: Refinement of detail |
| --- | --- | --- | --- |
| | **Descriptors** | **Actions and emotions** | |
| 1: Preparing for the lesson | Confident, excited, aware of the time until the start. | Feel full of energy, confident in my ability. I can hear the students outside. | I am preparing for the start of the lesson. I am feeling energized, confident and ready to teach. |
| 2: Meet and greet | Greet students outside. Instructions as to the next lesson. | I go out and greet the students – I stand confidently and call them to attention. I feel alert and enthused. | I go outside pre-empting the bell so I am there before the students. I stand confidently, this is my classroom and it is my lesson. I will enjoy it with the students. I can hear the bell and see the students coming to line up. I tell them the instructions for entering the classroom and settling themselves. |

**Table 11.1**    (Continued)

| Phase 1: Basic awareness | Phase 2: Inclusion of details | | Phase 3: Refinement of detail |
| | Descriptors | Actions and Emotions | |
| --- | --- | --- | --- |
| 3: Transition | Position in classroom. Monitoring. | Position myself so I can monitor what is happening and be seen. | I enter the classroom first and wait by the door so I can monitor the students settling. I remind them what they need. |
| 4: Focusing students attention | Move to front of class. Ensure attention. Inform students of the first task. | I feel my heart increasing but this inspires me with confidence: this is my adrenaline to ensure I am on top form for the lesson. I move with confidence to the front of the class. | I walk comfortably and confidently to the front of my class. I face the students and ask for everyone to look forward. I am alert for those who may be distracted and call them to attention. I ask the students to write five questions on their whiteboards. |
| 5: Introductory task | Students complete task. Start timer on board. | I am relaxed yet focused on the students. I am aware of what I want to ask them next. | All of the students are actively engaged with writing their questions. I start the time on the board. I monitor their engagement. I will ask students to swap boards with a partner when the time is up. |

## Practising imagery before the event

Mental practice is essential. After deciding on whether to use internal or external imagery, you should consider another aspect of imagery, related to the job that you want imagery to help you with. *You need to decide whether your imagery needs to be a general or specific sequence. Then you need to decide whether you need it for cognitive or motivational reasons.* If it is to do with teaching strategy, it will be cognitive. If it is to do with boosting confidence, for example, it will be motivational. Table 11.2 will help you in deciding which type of mental imagery you may need.

Having decided which imagery to use, you are now ready to practise. This is where we must return to the issue of controlling the mental imagery sequence. We would ask you to return to the 'living room' sequence discussed earlier, but this time, to imagine a friend or colleague sitting on one of the chairs. We would then make suggestions about that

**Table 11.2** Different types of mental imagery

|  | Cognitive/instructional | Motivational |
|---|---|---|
| General | **Strategic planning**<br>e.g. imaging a strategy to gain students' attention and maintain it for the start of the lesson. | **Arousal**<br>e.g. imaging increases or decreases in heart rate before the lesson. |
| Specific | **Skills-practise**<br>e.g. imaging the fine balance between helping individuals and monitoring the class. | **Goal-response**<br>e.g. imaging students achieving the lesson outcomes and ending the lesson on time in a calm manner. |

*Source*: Adapted from Paivio, 1985

person: are they smiling; drinking a cup of coffee; how are they sitting and so on? Next, we would ask you to imagine the person getting up and walking over to switch on the television. You should be able to control what is happening within the imagery sequence. In developing control, it is then necessary, for example, for you to imagine an anxiety-evoking situation from your teaching. This might be a situation such as the moments leading up to the start of a lesson. Perhaps you may focus on the 'feelings' of anxiety: tension in the shoulders and neck; increased heart rate; dry mouth; clammy hands. We would then take each of these and ask you to imagine the shoulders and neck becoming more relaxed, the speed of the heart beat reducing, saliva beginning to return in the mouth, and perspiration on the hands beginning to dry. *If you have been able to focus on these things returning to normal, YOU have controlled all the things causing heightened anxiety and are now ready to focus on the lesson.* The power of verbalizing the situation will prepare you for the lesson when it happens in reality. Your imagery practice should enhance your positive emotions (McCarthy, 2009). As we have pointed out throughout this chapter, the key word of course is, *'practise'*!

## Practising imagery after the event

Although this seems rather strange, practising imagery sequences after a lesson is a useful technique. It can act as a kind of debrief to ensure that the imagery used before the event was appropriate. If you find that certain things didn't go according to plan, or there were unexpected situations that arose, then now is the time to incorporate this new information before it gets forgotten. Is it for cognitive/instructional or motivational reasons? This will enhance your store of information about this particular situation for next time. (Please note that in the previous chapter we warned about using this technique directly after one lesson and before another due to the impact on focus.)

> 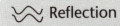 **Reflection**
>
> Consider an event that happened which you would like to revisit. Replay the event in your mind bringing it to the conclusion you wish to have achieved.

## Imagery scripts

Having developed your first written imagery script, you might now be considering variations on it, to cover different situations within the same lesson. Perhaps the students had more trouble understanding the concept. Perhaps they completed their work before you had envisaged. What would you then do? You will begin to build up an actual set of electronic or paper copies of your sequences. Keep them together in a file for reference purposes and for review if you need to return to them to refresh your memory. Think of this file as being a recipe book of lessons, or strategies to incorporate for different scenarios.

## Contextual setting

Wherever possible, you should aim to carry out your mental imagery sequence in a contextually appropriate setting, such as in the classroom. Of course such an enriched environment will also serve to be motivational (Beadle, 2008). ***This will provide an element of reality.***

Research by Godden and Baddeley (1975) reveals that recall from memory works well if it takes place in the same environment in which it was learned, known as context-dependent memory. The same applies to the 'state' that you are in when you learn. If you are relaxed when you learn, you will remember more if you are relaxed when tested, but if you are tense, you will not be able to remember as much. We flippantly tell our students that if they revise for an examination when they are drunk, the theory suggests that they should remember more in the examination if they are drunk! Of course, we swiftly move on to point out the obvious flaw in this argument! In psychology, there are always exceptions to the rule!

## Contextual props

If you are unable to carry out your mental imagery sequence at the school, perhaps because you are developing it before you even get there, then there are things that you can do to enhance the sequence (for example, recall our comment about odour-evoked memories). For instance, you may have a different wardrobe for teaching than from your casual clothes. Put your teaching clothes on and run through the mental imagery sequence in your mind. We're sure you will agree that it feels so much more 'real'. Other contextual props could be identified but we would rather you consider what is significant for your own script.

## One-minute summary

In this chapter we have discussed what mental imagery is, possible theories underlying it, and its use in different situations and for different reasons. We have gone on to explain how to set up a bank of imagery sequences and suggested ways of practising and refining these sequences.

We suggest that you practise each element of imagery (general; specific; cognitive/instructional; motivational) so that you can master each one. You never know when a new challenge will emerge and, if practise in one element is lacking, it always seems to be in the area that is needed at this very moment in time! Of course, it takes time to develop imagery sequences that work but we would argue that the time devoted to such practice would pay dividends in the long run. In the next chapter, we move on to the topic of resilience.

## Short-term strategies for the here and now

- Consider one small element that you may continually worry about or have problems with. Consider the various stages within the area through analysing each step. Work through Table 11.1 in order to develop the process and how you could react.
- Develop a simple mental imagery script:
  - Start with the basics. Use imagery that will be simple but effective.
  - Don't overcomplicate it. Build it from scratch and then add to it.
  - Don't try to picture intricacies of classroom management if you can't visualize walking around the classroom, seeing the displays, the resources, hearing the noise outside, and so on.
  - If you can see the classroom, then add the visual complexities (like the peeling paint under the radiator).
  - If you can see this, then add more detail … Finally if you can do all this, you can focus on responding to a student who is not focused on their work.
  - Picture the scene in your mind, the class, the other students, the lesson. Now picture the student losing focus and starting to distract others.
  - Run through your mind what you would do in this situation and how your actions bring about a resolution.

- Once you are familiar with using the technique, make a list of occasions for which you might write an imagery script. Again, avoid confining this resource to the classroom. You may mentally rehearse an upcoming job interview for head of department, a new post elsewhere, or a difficult negotiation with a colleague. The list is almost endless.

## Mentoring issues

Discussing a lesson they have just observed with a mentor will allow you to try out the imagery. They may have highlighted something you were unaware of. To this extent, they may be able to offer advice on the appropriate action. Perhaps they have suggested that you may want to consider transition between tasks. Whatever the focus, this is a perfect time to put your imagery script into practice.

Similarly, you may want to ask a mentor to observe a specific part of the lesson which you have worked on using your imagery skills. What is their feedback? Has imagery helped?

## Further reading

Gawain, S. (2002) *Creative Visualization: Use the Power of Your Imagination to Create What You Want in Your Life*. Novato, CA: New World Library.
This could perhaps be referred to as a 'pop-psychology' book although one of the more useful and practical books available.

Joffe, V.L., Cain, K. and Maric, N. (2007) 'Comprehension problems in children with specific language impairment: does *mental imagery* training help?', *International Journal of Language & Communication Disorders*, 42(6): 648–64.
This paper explores the use of mental imagery in helping children who are struggling with comprehension and reading. The findings show that using *mental imagery* is effective in boosting the story comprehension of children with specific language impairment.

Lazarus, A.A. (1984) *In the Mind's Eye*. New York: Guilford Press.
A dated book but one which is continually referred to as authoritative and useful.

McCarthy, P.J. (2009) 'Putting imagery to good affect: a case study among youth swimmers', *Sport and Exercise Psychology Review*, 5(1): 27–38.
This paper explores how imagery can be used to enhance positive emotions.

Taktek, K., Zinsser, N. and St-John, B. (2008) 'Visual versus kinaesthetic mental imagery: efficacy for the retention and transfer of a closed motor skill in young children', *Canadian Journal of Experimental Psychology*, 62(3): 174–87.

This paper compares the effects in young children of visual versus kinaesthetic mental imagery and physical practice on the retention and transfer of throwing a ball (with the non-dominant hand) at a target. Read it to see what the findings were (and as usual, don't be put off by the 'academic jargon').

Van Toller, S. and Dodd, G.H. (eds) (1993) *Fragrance: Psychology and Biology of Perfume.* London: Springer Verlag.

Van Toller, S. (2009) *The Nose and I.* (Forthcoming.)

Vroon, P. (1997) *Smell: The Secret Seducer.* New York: FSG
If you have a keen interest in the sense of smell, these books will provide further detail. The Van Toller and Dodd book is a collection of academic, yet accessible papers written by researchers across the globe. The Vroon book may be used as a 'starting point' for more in-depth reading.

# 12

# When the Going Gets Tough … ! Mental Resilience

| Chapter contents | Page |
|---|---|

## Introduction

Mental resilience is about overcoming anxiety and fear in stressful situations. It is about the will to 'go that extra mile', the ability to 'keep going' when you are flagging, to continue to endure in an attempt to achieve a goal. A general definition which helps to identify key elements of mental resilience is, 'The ability to stand tall in the face of adversity ... a psychic resiliency that allows you to rebound from setbacks and failures time and time again' (Loehr, 1995: 11). You can accept poor performance as a failing in yourself and your skill; alternately you can view it as a test of your capability. So, mental resilience is about endurance and stamina. It is completely psychological. It is based only in the head of the teacher. Mental resilience for one person will not necessarily be the same as mental resilience for another person. It is therefore unique to each individual. This is why people can give up before they have even started. So, all you need to do is read this chapter and then you will have all the answers on how to become mentally tough ... well, not quite! In this chapter, we will provide guidance on aspects of psychological functioning that may help you to highlight what mental resilience means to you. We will refer to many of the other chapters in this book and show you that mental resilience is more of a culmination of elements, rather like the pieces in a jigsaw puzzle that should help to create the overall 'picture' that is mental resilience. If there were to be a single piece that is bigger than any other, we would perhaps argue that this is 'self-confidence'. Without self-confidence, it is virtually impossible to develop or maintain mental resilience.

Surely, the simple answer is to read the chapter on self-confidence to solve the problem. Again, not quite! Self-confidence may be the largest piece in the jigsaw, but is itself made up of many smaller pieces. So, we are back to square one. The key to issues of mental resilience and self-confidence lies in reading this book, identifying areas to work on and developing steadily over time.

## Chapter objectives

- Consider how a unified approach of the strategies covered enables mental resilience.
- Understand the use of performance profiling.
- Develop your own performance profile.
- Complete the mental resilience questionnaire.
- Understand how to control and channel thoughts and feelings.
- Use an 'energizing' mental imagery script.

## Restructuring your mental DNA

In order to acquire mental resilience, it will be necessary to work through any of the factors that you believe are missing from your 'mental DNA'. Using mental DNA as an analogy suggests that resilience is made up of component parts and all we need to do is obtain these parts, assemble them and then incorporate them into our genetic make-up. Of course, we are not suggesting that we can change our genetic code. But we do have an image in our mind of creating a psychological profile that is adapted to 'survive', fitting appropriately with Charles Darwin's 'survival of the fittest'.

In working through the chapters in this book, you will be getting closer and closer to assembling all of the ingredients necessary for you to be psychologically strong when previously you may have started to flag. If you are confident that you have a wide range of skills and techniques to help you through any challenge, you will be more likely to move into 'the zone' for teaching, a different level of consciousness where everything seems effortless. We will lead on to this later in the next chapter, when we talk about 'flow' states.

The initial question is therefore, 'how do you know what the component parts of mental resilience are and whether or not you possess them?' One way of finding out is by using the technique of performance profiling, which we have used many times with teachers, to great effect.

## Performance profiling

A simple yet effective method of identifying missing elements in your mental DNA is through the use of performance profiling. Performance profiling was developed for sport by Butler and Hardy in 1992. It has since been used to good effect in identifying mental resilience in sports such as soccer and cricket. In our opinion, its use is ideal in helping discover a teacher's perception of his or her physical, technical and psychological abilities at the present time. Completing the performance profile is a three-step process. *First, you should think of a teacher whom you would aspire to emulate*.

There is no right or wrong answer here. Having identified the 'target person', *the second step is to write down a list of qualities that you think the teacher has that made them so special*. It is also important to write down what you mean by those qualities, since you may not remember exactly what you meant if you look back a few months later. The response sheet in Table 12.1 will provide a template for you to do this.

**Activity 12.1**

You will have come across many teachers either when you attended school as a child, or teachers you have worked with through your training and practice. List these. Who was the most influential? Why?

List the positive attributes from all of the teachers you have identified. Develop a composite image of a teacher who encompasses all of these attributes. Consider how they are all attributes you are capable of achieving.

To give some examples, perhaps you think that resilience is an important part of the teacher you wish to emulate. The meaning of 'resilience' for you might be the ability to keep trying to improve the learning ability of your students. Alternatively, it might be the ability to ensure you provide 100 per cent commitment to the pile of marking you are faced with, where each is marked with the same level of care. So, the definition can change even if the word stays the same. Another example quality would perhaps be 'concentration', which we might define as regaining focus after teaching a specifically challenging lesson. Or, perhaps we might define it as retaining a high level of attention for the whole of the teaching week. As we said, there is no right or wrong, it is merely our perception.

In Table 12.1 we have put this into context through developing a performance profile. In the first column, we have listed the quality to develop, concentration. In column 2, we have provided our meaning for this word. From this, we have provided a rating in column 3 of how high we think the 'ideal teacher' we have in mind exhibits this quality. This is scored on a 1–10 rating, where 10 is the highest. In the example, we have put the 'ideal teacher' as 9. The fourth column is where we put our personal rating – for the example, we have rated as 3. Consequently, this provides information on where we want to be ... and where we are now in terms of concentration. All (and we use the word loosely) we have to do is to find a way of reaching 9 out of 10. The performance profile has thus highlighted a goal to be pursued. Chapter 8 on goal setting provides

**Table 12.1**  Example performance profile record sheet

| Quality | Meaning | Ideal rating (1–10) | Current rating (1–10) | Goals/strategies to improve |
|---------|---------|---------------------|------------------------|------------------------------|
| Concentration | Ability to stay focused after a challenging lesson | 9 | 3 | Self-talk to keep myself focused. Mental imagery to run through how the lesson could have been different. |

detailed guidance on how to achieve this: in the example, we have detailed the various strategies we could consider in the final column.

 **Activity 12.2**

Complete the performance profile record sheet as detailed below.

**Performance Profile Record Sheet**

Think about a teacher whom you admire and consider the qualities the teacher possesses that allows them to produce the performances you admire. The quality could be within one of three categories:

- Knowledge and understanding
- Strategic
- Psychological

Identify one of the qualities that you consider you need to develop. Write this in the first column.

Consider the meaning of the quality as it applies to your perspective. Write this in the second column.

In the third column, give the 'ideal teacher' a score of 1 (lowest) to 10 (highest). In the fourth column, provide your personal rating for this quality from 1 to 10.

In the final column, consider how you could use goal setting or strategies to develop this quality.

| Quality | Meaning | Ideal rating (1–10) | Current rating (1–10) | Goals/strategies to improve |
|---------|---------|---------------------|-----------------------|------------------------------|
|         |         |                     |                       |                              |

## Interpreting the performance profile

As you can see from the record sheet, the teacher is guided towards splitting the required qualities into three separate categories: knowledge and understanding, strategic, and psychological. We recommend that you do this for two reasons. First, it provides some clues as to what is required. Many teachers struggle with the performance profile if they are not given some help in starting to complete the record sheet. Of course, there is a fine balance to be reached between making suggestions to the teacher, on the one hand, and putting 'words in their mouth', on the other hand. The performance profile is self-focused (it is your own opinion of what is needed to be successful in teaching) and as such, completing it should be a self-focused activity (it should be about you). By providing three possible categories, we offer a foundation upon which to build and, therefore, guide you in making a start.

It goes without saying that a psychologist is expecting to see a list of psychological qualities with which they can work. Although this is obviously where they are looking to provide support and guidance, it is only half of the story. We are not necessarily experts in the curriculum area or key stage that you work in. Nevertheless, we believe that it is important to focus on more than just the psychological elements underlying possible 'challenges'. When we interpret performance profiles, we look to the psychological factors but also pay attention to the other qualities of knowledge/ understanding and strategic qualities appearing on the record sheet. It may be that a theme emerges. We might implement a goal-setting programme that helps to provide focus and this has a knock-on effect with the teacher's confidence. There may be more factors that are indicating a particular theme and the rule of thumb is that the more factors that emerge, the greater the likelihood that the problem, or 'challenge' (as we would prefer to call it) can be confirmed. This prevents being sidetracked or taking an inappropriate course of action, only to discover that the problem is still present. The message therefore is to carefully consider the possible interrelationships between the qualities that you write down and keep an open mind when interpreting the performance profile. It is there to help you, not to throw challenges at you.

The example quality, 'concentration', that we provided on the record sheet is purely for illustrative purposes. Equally, the meaning we have provided may be personal to ourselves. If you write the same quality in column 1, it is important for you to clarify its meaning. Two teachers might both therefore consider concentration to be important to their teaching, but both might think of it in different terms. For teacher 1, concentration could be as we have described it, 'The ability to stay focused after a particularly challenging lesson'. For teacher 2, concentration could be, 'Thinking about my teaching strategy being prepared to adapt it if necessary'. Here we have two completely different interpretations of the word 'concentration' (neither of which may coincide with a dictionary definition!). The advice and guidance that we would give to teacher 1 would be useless for teacher 2 and vice versa. For teacher 1, we would perhaps investigate the reasons why concentration is lost after the lesson. One might think that this would be obvious, but psychologists do not jump to conclusions. A different teacher might not be distracted by such a lesson and may instead perceive it simply as their lack of preparation. Yet for teacher 1, it appears to be causing a major distraction. In contrast, for teacher 2, we might perhaps explore whether they are using imagery to consider alternate approaches. Having identified the source of the problem, a solution can be suggested through one or more of the techniques outlined in the practical chapters. The same word, 'concentration', does not necessarily mean that the same problem is being experienced or that the same solution will be successful.

## Low scores: a *caveat*

Once the record sheet and profile have been produced, it is important that you deflect attention away from the negative points, in favour of the positive ones. It is easy for a teacher to see the 'low scores' and interpret these as a sign of failure. This, of course, is not the reality of the situation.

Rather, we tend to suggest to teachers that this should provide them with an opportunity to see marked improvements on these scores over a period of time, a point that we will deal with shortly. Low scores may therefore be seen in a positive way. Seeing improvements, for example, from a 1 to a 4 and on to a 7 should raise self-esteem, self-confidence and, thus, performance.

## Strengths and challenges: a *caveat*

The initial focus after interpreting the performance profile may be to prioritize some of the 'qualities' where you need to make progress. We would always advise against focusing on too many of these at one time, since to do so may have detrimental effects. So we tend to recommend writing down three strengths and three 'challenges' to begin working on.

There is, however, a word of warning. As we have commented previously, it is human nature not to look at oneself for faults but rather to blame others for failings. A similar principle can be applied to performance profiling. We have heard the comment many times, 'I will work on the three strengths to get them from a 7 to a 9 or 10.' Every time this comment is made to us, what we actually hear is, 'I would rather stick my head in the sand and pretend the problem isn't there!' It is far easier to work on things that one is already accomplished in, than do the hard work in developing the things that one is not so adept at accomplishing. So, when the three challenges are listed, it is important for you to focus on and discuss ways in which progress can be made. It is actually quite common to discover that by working on the low scores, the higher scores also increase, having a knock-on effect on the teacher's performance overall.

## Performance profiles over a period of time

The frequency with which you should complete a performance profile will depend on certain things. One of these is the urgency of showing progress in overcoming the problem. If you keep losing self-confidence, it is important to focus on this aspect of the profile in order to keep confidence levels as high as possible. A second consideration should be availability of time. Teachers are increasingly busy and time is, therefore, a precious commodity.

Completing a performance profile on a regular basis adds to the activities on a teacher's agenda. However, it is important that you allocate an appropriate amount of time to this. After setting up the qualities and meanings initially, the technique is no longer time consuming. Allow half an hour to complete the initial work and then 5 to 10 minutes every time you wish to update the scores.

In answering the question of how often to complete a performance profile?, we would recommend sufficiently long enough to see a difference, but not so long that motivation to make progress diminishes. This answer is of little use at one level, however, it illustrates the fact that teachers are individuals and, consequently, we cannot be more specific than saying that you should complete a performance profile regularly. This may be four months apart, every half-term or even every week. Personal preference plays a role here. A teacher, in discussion with their mentor, must select a 'window of opportunity' when completing their performance profile to maximize its effectiveness.

## Performance profiling: why so late in the book?

If performance profiling is so important in providing beneficial information on a teacher's current profile, you might wonder why it appears so late on in the book. This is completely intentional!

First, there is little point in asking you to evaluate your current psychological profile if you are unaware of the kind of themes that may be influencing that profile. In face-to-face circumstances, a psychologist has the luxury of being able to discuss issues with the teacher and explore elements of the teacher's psyche. It is not possible to do this through prose in a book. Under these circumstances, it is the information contained in this book that should guide you in questioning yourself effectively. *Having gained knowledge from the preceding chapters, you are now in an informed position to begin to think about your own profile and the kind of elements in your own 'toolkit' that require development*.

Secondly, although you are nearing the end of the book, you are in fact nearing the start of your journey of discovery. The performance profile can act to inform you of where you want to end up (that is, through the ideal rating). Think of it as being a road map to a destination (it won't be long before the students you have taught ask, 'What's a road map?' – the analogy just doesn't seem to work so well with the term 'sat nav' instead!).

Performance profiling can be used for all sorts of things. Indeed we could have completed our own performance profile, before embarking on this book. We could have considered the qualities required to complete the project, our strengths and challenges, our skills and areas where we may lack expertise, before setting goals to develop our profiles into that of 'author'. If you 'think outside the box', you can use performance profiling to your advantage. This is another area that we believe is directly transferable to your students in the classroom. Teach then how to solve problems by setting those problems in relation to performance profiles. We would be keen to hear from those of you that do try this with your students.

In terms of mental resilience, however, performance profiling only serves as a starting point and does not provide all the information you might require, so you will need to complement it with some questionnaire data and it is to this that we will now turn.

## Mental resilience questionnaire

If you want to collect personal information to see how strong you might be mentally for the start of a term, then you have to go down the route of the mental resilience questionnaire.

Various questionnaires for measuring mental resilience exist and we will introduce one of these here which has been adapted significantly from Loehr's 'Mental Toughness Test' to apply to teaching (Activity 12.3). In order not to bias a teacher's responses, we would usually ask them to complete one of these, in conjunction with a performance profile, before debriefing them.

| Activity 12.3 | Yes | No |
|---|---|---|
| Do you see yourself as more of a success than a failure in teaching? | | |
| Do you believe in yourself as a teacher? | | |
| Do you remain confident when things are not going your way? | | |
| Can you perform toward the upper range of your talent and skill? | | |

*(Continued)*

*(Continued)*

| Activity 12.3 | Yes | No |
|---|---|---|
| *If you have answered 'yes' your self-confidence may be high.* | | |
| Are you highly motivated to motivate yourself and do your best? | | |
| Do you set goals to keep you working hard as a teacher? | | |
| Are you prepared to give whatever it takes to reach your full potential as a teacher? | | |
| Do you wake up in the morning excited about teaching? | | |
| *If you have answered 'yes' your motivation may be high.* | | |
| Are you able to keep your focus during teaching? | | |
| Can you remain calm during teaching when faced with problems? | | |
| Are you able to clear interfering emotions quickly and regain your focus? | | |
| *If you have answered 'yes' your attentional control may be high.* | | |
| Are you able to think positively during teaching? | | |
| Do you give 100 per cent effort during teaching, no matter what? | | |
| Are you able to change negative moods into positive ones by controlling your thinking? | | |
| Can you turn 'crisis' into 'opportunity'? | | |
| *If you have answered 'yes' your ability to control your attitude may be high.* | | |
| Are you able to keep strong positive emotion flowing during teaching? | | |
| Do you enjoy teaching even when you face lots of difficult problems? | | |
| Do you get inspired for the challenge in tough situations? | | |

| Activity 12.3 | Yes | No |
|---|---|---|
| Does teaching give you a genuine sense of joy and fulfilment? | | |
| *If you have answered 'yes' your 'positive energy' may be high.* | | |
| Are you able to visualize yourself teaching successfully? | | |
| Are you able to mentally rehearse your teaching skills? | | |
| Do you visualize working through challenging situations prior to a lesson? | | |
| Do you use imagery before beginning an important lesson to help you perform better? | | |
| *If you have answered 'yes' your ability to control mental imagery may be high.* | | |
| Do you get angry and frustrated when teaching? | | |
| Do you get nervous or afraid when teaching? | | |
| Do mistakes get you feeling and thinking negatively? | | |
| Do your muscles become overly tight when teaching? | | |
| *If you have answered 'No' your ability to minimize 'negative energy' may be high (low negative energy is a good thing).* | | |

These sections may be the 'ingredients' of mental resilience. If you have all of the right ingredients, there is a strong likelihood that you will be a successful teacher. If you don't have these ingredients, you can obtain them with the help of this book, guidance from mentors and further reading around the discipline of introductory psychology. Our website will provide supplementary guidance.

## Interpreting mental resilience information

For psychologists, interpreting mental resilience questionnaires is quite straightforward. The skill lies in reaching a solution based on the information obtained. The questions above, alongside the performance profile aim to draw out the type of information covered by the preceding chapters of this book and show that mental resilience is a combination of many separate, yet interrelated elements.

When we work with teachers, our aim is to use these techniques to collect data, from which we can explore emerging themes, needs and, subsequently, solutions. If the two types of information gathering do not concur with each other, this does not mean that discrepancies exist, but merely that the 'issues' may be less pronounced and in need of further exploration. Let's face it, the human mind is extremely complicated and the 'quick fix' is rarely a panacea for all 'ills'.

## Practical techniques to improve mental resilience

In running sessions on mental resilience with teachers, we usually ask teachers to tell us how they normally react to 'adverse' situations, for example:

- Following a cycle of inconsistent performance.
- Following a distracted incident involving poor decision-making.
- Continuing to lose focus or the motivation to complete a specific task.

The key to mental resilience is 'positive optimism', a term used to describe thinking in positive terms and seeing problems as challenges rather than as problems. Positive optimism can be achieved by:

- Becoming aware of yourself and your body.
- Knowing the ideal performance state and being able to adjust this when necessary.
- Controlling/channelling thoughts and feelings.

We favour three techniques that will help you to achieve positive optimism and enhance mental resilience, listed below. You will see how important they are when you work through the practical example below.

## Disciplined positive thinking

You should practise positive thinking and positive imagery with the underlying pretext that negative thinking leads to negative performance, both of which reflect a lack of self-discipline and undermine your attempts to think positively. Think along the lines of forming a habit of positive thinking and imagery.

## Channelling thoughts and feelings

You should familiarize yourself with continually identifying and attempting to change negative thoughts and feelings to positive ones, by taking control of your thought processes (as shown in Chapter 10 on self-talk). Thinking energetically also transfers to performance in a positive way (see the energy script below). Practise thinking quickly and making quick confident decisions without changing your mind, then quickly evaluating your progress so that the positive thoughts and successful ongoing performance will reinforce the fact that you are 'doing the job'. Sometimes humour can help to immediately relieve a stressful situation. Think about a situation that you thought was funny, because you made a simple 'basic mistake'. As soon as you make light of it, it becomes less intense and you will feel better. Alternatively, if you have made a serious error of judgement, try to find the humour in it somewhere. You will minimize its impact just by trivializing it. Of course, you still need to examine the underlying problem, just don't do it at this moment in time when you need to channel your thoughts and feelings into 'getting on with the challenge'.

## Prioritizing positive and negative self-talk

You should be aware of and accept that negative thoughts and feelings sometimes occur when there is a 'challenge' to be met (a sort of 'no pain, no gain' philosophy). You should explore the 'challenge' and identify whether this is something which can be solved immediately or which should be sidelined until a more appropriate moment.

## An example 'energizing' mental imagery script

Using a number of strategies we have detailed in this book, the script in Table 12.2 (overleaf) combines breathing and mental imagery to help 'energize' when you may be flagging.

 **Activity 12.4**

Give this script a go!

Please note, as is usual with mental imagery scripts, some people find that they can't stop laughing at first because the wording

*(Continued)*

*(Continued)*

sounds so ridiculously funny. This is quite normal! If this happens to you, simply try to follow the instructions by concentrating a little harder. You will get into the rhythm fairly quickly and will then reap the benefits.

Read it through several times so that you are aware of the various stages, otherwise you can download the MP3 file from the website.

Be aware after completing the exercise of any feelings you have in your mind or in your body. Make a note of these.

**Table 12.2**    Energizing mental imagery script

| Step | Instruction |
| --- | --- |
| 1 | Find a quiet environment where you can make yourself comfortable. |
| 2 | Close your eyes and allow yourself to focus on your breathing. |
| 3 | When you feel focused and calm transfer your thoughts to your abdomen. |
| 4 | Imagine a ball of pure energy in your abdomen, which can move around your body when you control it. |
| 5 | As the energy ball travels down and then up your right leg it leaves behind a trace of pure energy which your muscles can use. |
| 6 | This energy ball then travels slowly down and up your left leg then back to your abdomen. |
| 7 | The energy ball then travels up and down your arms one at a time and back to your abdomen. |
| 8 | After energizing your limbs all your thoughts should focus on your powerful and precise movements. |
| 9 | Break off a piece of this energy ball and send it up towards your head. |
| 10 | When it reaches your brain, all your thoughts become sharp, focused and your decisions become quick and precise. |
| 11 | Bring yourself back to the present, by counting from 10 down to 1 and remind yourself how you feel refreshed, full of energy and mentally strong enough to take on any challenge that the day throws at you. |

*Source*: Adapted from West, 2005

If you are unsure when to use a script of this type, we would suggest that sitting in the classroom, focusing on the first lesson, would be an ideal time to be experiencing the 'energy ball' flowing around your body mentally. As the bell sounds for the start of the day, the energy explodes and you burst into action, fully prepared for the day and mentally strong.

You may need to 're-energize' during the day. Let's imagine that you are beginning to drop off the pace at lunchtime. What better time to use the 'energy ball' tactic, providing you with an instant burst of pace.

With practice, even just thinking about the 'energy ball' will be enough, because you will have trained your brain to associate the mental image with mental strength.

## A final comment

Having acquired various 'pieces of the jigsaw' you can, with the guidance offered in these chapters, concentrate on putting those pieces together to form the complete picture. This may take some time or it may happen very quickly. When it happens should be of less importance. What is more important, however, is that it does happen. In the final chapter, we will draw each of the strands of this book together and welcome you to the beginning of your 'new' way of thinking about teaching and what to do to help you to slip 'into the zone' of optimal functioning, where teaching seems to be effortless.

## One-minute summary

Mental resilience unites a number of the practical psychological skills training techniques described in the last few chapters. The key to developing your potential is to identify a focus through performance profiling, noting where you currently are and where you would like to progress to. Ensuring that you keep referring back to the profile in order to monitor your progress and identify areas for further progress will help ensure you continue to hone your developing skills.

## Short-term strategies for the here and now

- Complete a performance profile record sheet (Activity 12.2).
- Run through the energizing mental imagery script (Table 12.2).
- Answer the mental resilience questions in Activity 12.3 to identify any potential areas that are causing specific challenges.
- From this, consult the relevant chapter in this book as identified with each block of related questions.

## Mentoring issues

Discuss the use of your performance profiling sheet with your mentor. The key aspect is for you to identify the areas for improvement, perhaps with suggestions from your mentor. However, the scores that you allocate for each area you want to work on should be your honest and subjective scores.

# 📖 Further reading

Sarma, K. (2008) *Mental Resilience: The Power of Clarity: How to Develop the Focus of a Warrior and the Peace of a Monk*. Novato, CA: New World Library.
This book combines Eastern and Western traditions in order to survive the modern world. We particularly like the appeal of the warrior-monk paradox throughout this readable book.

# Section 4

## Epilogue

The final chapter is in part a reminder of how this book is integrated to facilitate your success in the classroom. Yet how is success measured? We explore this in relation to the personally rewarding construct of 'flow', where everything seems to happen in an effortless manner. The paradox is that it takes effort to become effortless! The effort we discuss is through engaging with the various activities and reflections contained in this book.

# 13

# The Final Bell ... the Journey Begins

## Introduction

The title of this chapter suggests that having read the previous chapters, a teacher is now completely equipped to be the best they can become. Of course, this is not the reality of the situation. This chapter highlights the fact that this is only the beginning. In the preceding chapters, we have provided the necessary 'tools of the trade' to do the job. As with all of us, when we initially use any tools, we are rather 'ham-fisted' until we understand that there is a certain 'technique' to using these tools successfully. Psychological skills are no different. This chapter provides guidance on developing these skills to the point where they can be used successfully time and time again and suggests a way forward on the road to psychological success.

## Chapter objectives

- Understand how changing your perspective can motivate even when feeling 'stuck'.
- Identify the 'flow' state and understand how this may be achieved.
- Consider how flow can be intrinsically rewarding.

## Build on sound foundations: Rome wasn't built in a day

We would never advocate trying to use any of the techniques or advice in this book without practising them beforehand. There is little point in trying a new technique for the first time when your reputation is at stake. Rather, you should begin by practising them when the stakes are low, then begin to implement them during your day-to-day teaching activities, before evaluating and refining them. We have heard the comment on many occasions, 'Well I tried it for a day or two and it didn't work.' Our response is usually something along the lines of, 'Well, do you think you gave it sufficient time for it to work?' Give the techniques time to work effectively.

## Be prepared to struggle before you succeed

It is essential to be aware of a possible dip in performance before an improvement occurs. As with any piece of 'new' resource or strategy, a teacher needs to get used to the way it changes their teaching. If you acquire a new psychological skill, the case is no different. While you are developing the psychological skill, it may feel as if you are going backwards yet, with practice, you will begin to improve and your performance will enter the next level. So, the message is, *be prepared to struggle before you succeed*. Of course, this will not always be the case. On many occasions, the psychological skill can have an immediate, positive effect on performance, or at least, your feelings about performance. The message is simple. *You must practise these psychological skills well in advance of the time that you need them most!*

## 'Staleness': Are you in a rut or on a plateau?

There will be times when you reach a stage beyond which you just cannot seem to go. Again, this is a common situation to find yourself in and is not a problem. Indeed, acknowledging having reached a 'rut' or a 'plateau' is vital to progress. Too many teachers avoid looking at themselves when progress is not being made. There is almost a sense of 'familiarity' beyond which we don't wish to extend ourselves. Through this book, you should be open and honest with yourself, acknowledge when you may be stuck and begin searching for a solution. This may involve, for example, changing aspects of your teaching style, concentration strategy or relaxation routine.

A rut is a hole. If you view the situation as a rut, then negative psychological connotations will take hold. You would have to climb out of a rut, a difficult thing to do perhaps and certainly something involving action on your behalf. On the other hand, a plateau is plain. It implies that you have embarked on a climb and reached a wide expanse of land with various directions to proceed. If you view the situation as a plateau the problem presents itself more as a 'choice'. Which direction shall you go in and what resources will you need to reach your destination. Suddenly, you have created 'opportunities', rather than 'difficulties', just by thinking about the situation differently and you need to evaluate your options in order to make your decision on which direction to head off in. In short, you are adopting an active role in decision-making.

The plateau metaphor works nicely in teaching. We have spoken to many teachers who, when faced with a plateau, try harder and harder to overcome the problem and end up making the situation worse because they are trying too hard. Our advice would be to take a step back, assess the situation, use the techniques offered in this book, and ask the 'how' question: 'How do I ... ?' The teacher is then looking for solutions rather than barriers.

 ## Activity 13.1

Previously we have noted the importance of mental imagery. The same can be applied here. Look for a picture which appeals to you, one that has some wide open expanse with peaks in the background. It may be a holiday photograph, or it could be a picture you have found on the Internet. If it has personal symbolism, even better.

Consider how peaceful and serene the plateau is. Consider the 'journey' it may have taken to have reached the plateau. The plateau thus serves as a resting place ... somewhere to gather your resources before you proceed further with your journey.

You may want to add a motivational quote to the picture ... one that appeals is Lao-Tzu's 'A journey of a thousand miles starts with a single step'. Of course you can either make your own quote, or take one that again holds personal meaning for you.

## Explore your commitment

Commitment is vital if you are to be, or remain successful within teaching. What actually drives teachers to remain in the profession for all of their working lives, as opposed to those who 'give up' after two or three years? The answer lies in commitment. Be careful here. Consider the teacher who has strived to complete their teacher training, with the many challenges in the way to reach that goal and their first job. Despite the challenges, they have 'made it' with their commitment and determination, along the way receiving good quality feedback about their placements. Yet into the job, their performance starts to plummet. In evaluating what is going wrong, we might explore the issue of commitment. Again, honesty is the key. Questioning your own commitment is painful at the best of times, let alone telling someone else. We would suggest that you minimize the 'pain' by getting used to being open and honest. If you do question your commitment, you have made an important step forward on the road to change.

This may be as simple as not having a strategy or set of process or performance goals for the current term. It is almost as if, 'I have achieved my goal ... now what?' Our advice, again, would be to focus on smaller elements of teaching rather than the 'bigger picture' in order to regain composure and return to the outstanding performance they are capable of.

## Give yourself rewards

We mentioned rewards in the chapter on goal setting. It is important for teachers to reward themselves when things are going well. It is equally important to do this when things are not going so well. This is perhaps a strange thing to say. But in fact, it is not as strange as it appears. If you are struggling, then you need to look for the smallest of improvements or positive elements in your teaching. For example, the day may have been one where nothing went right: you should then reward yourself with a few words of congratulation for doing a good job in the face of adversity, for surviving until the final bell. Always look for the positive elements and give yourself a pat on the back. Beware of rewards that may take your focus away. If you focus purely on those weeks of holidays that people outside teaching are envious of (if only they knew the truth!) your focus is taken away from the job of teaching. Focus on the job: provide yourself with a 'personal pat-on-the back' or 'time-for-an-activity' rewards while avoiding the materialistic, externally provided rewards. If you focus on such materialistic rewards, you may have a lovely furnished house with lots of gadgets, and so on, but also hefty debts to add to your burden. Focus on why you teach and why you went into teaching in the first place and you will find your life beyond riches.

# Teaching in 'the zone': strive to get into a state of 'flow'

If all the ingredients are in the same place at the same time, a teacher will enter 'the zone'. The zone is a place where everything seems to be effortless. You seem to be able to teach without trying and the students are learning with enthusiasm. You complete your planning, preparation, assessment and still have a full weekend to yourself. You are poised, composed, and in a state where everything seems effortless, time seems to slow down, decisions can be made easily and everything that happens becomes second nature. These are signs that you are indeed in the zone or, in a state of flow, where performance is optimized.

In guiding teachers through the concept of flow, we usually begin by asking them to think of a time when everything seemed to gel or come together, where their performance oozed quality and they just knew that it was good. We then ask the teacher to recall it from memory, with the help of the information sheet below. The example provided in Activity 13.2 details one teacher's description of such a flow state.

 Activity 13.2

Read the following statement and information:

> When I've been most content with my performance, I have felt at one with the students, the lesson, the classroom ... everything. I was really tuned into what I was doing and knew exactly how I was going to teach the lesson. I knew I had it all under control and I was completely aware of what everyone else was doing. I was totally absorbed in my teaching. I thought, 'this is so cool' and I just taught. I was in complete control of the situation. It felt really good'.

This is an example of a flow state. The mindset that accompanies flow aids in pushing a person to his or her limits. The mind and body are in unison. Indeed, this state is one which is intrinsically motivating and rewarding – just being able to reach this state in our teaching is the ultimate 'buzz'.

In your journal, describe a similar state you have experienced. It does not necessarily have to be in relation to teaching: identify a time when everything just seemed to work together in an effortless manner.

Specifically describe the situation as fully as possible. Although we have listed the W5H1 questions, feel free to adapt or amend as necessary:

*(Continued)*

*(Continued)*

- When did it take place?
- Where did it take place?
- Who were you with?
- What happened in the lead up to the event?
- How did the experience start?
- Why do you think the experience took place? Has this changed you in any way?

As you recall these experiences, use as many senses as possible to help. Write down your thoughts, feelings and impressions of the experience, including how you felt afterwards.

## The components of flow

According to the work of Mihalyi Csikszentmihalyi (Csikszentmihalyi, 2000), there are a number of 'ingredients' or elements that correlate with the flow state, as detailed in Table 13.1.

**Table 13.1** Finding 'flow' through the strategies listed in this book

| Conditions of flow | Description | Example to facilitate each element |
| --- | --- | --- |
| Balance of challenge and skills | You must have the skills to be able to cope with the challenges. If the challenges 'outweigh' your skills, you will feel anxious. If your skills 'outweigh' the challenges, you will become bored. If the balance is 'right' you can experience the flow state. | Consider the various chapters in this book that discuss setting your own challenges for some aspect of improvement, for example, goal setting or mental resilience. Have you made the challenge 'too easy'? Will you become bored? Is it 'too hard', where you become anxious ... or is it 'just right'? |
| Clarity of goals | You should set clear goals in advance of the event. It is important that you know exactly what it is that you wish to achieve. Your goals should be SMART. If goals are clear, you will be able to focus attention on strategy and consequently, concentration should remain for the duration of the day. | Visualizing your performances in advance of the actual day is a useful way of focusing on clear goals. Chapter 8 will be useful in setting such goals. |
| Immediacy of feedback | If you can get feedback on how well you are performing in the moment, you can monitor your strategy. | You should be aware of what is happening moment by moment. Is your heart racing? If it is, take a few deep breaths. |

**Table 13.1**   (Continued)

| Conditions of flow | Description | Example to facilitate each element |
|---|---|---|
| *Characteristics of the flow experience* | | |
| Concentration/ absorption | It goes without saying that concentration is critical to a task. You should think only of the task in hand, the lesson, etc. Avoid thinking too far ahead. Rather think only of the moment. The aim is to become at one with your lesson and the students, inseparable. | Try to fully engage in the lesson. Don't think about what you should have done, or should be preparing for the next lesson. Concentrate on the here and now. |
| Sense of control | Ideally, you should have a sense of unlimited resources (whether these are personal or physical resources) that will allow you to cope with anything that presents itself during the course of your day. You should be able to control your performance and how you feel about it. You should have total composure. If you do not have unlimited resources, then you should use the resources you do have in a way that works for you. If you know you have resilience, for example, you should feel confident that this will shine through, towards the end of the day or the week, when other people may be getting tired or losing focus. A sense of control comes from your belief in your abilities. Avoid 'trying to gain control'. Instead, focus on what you are capable of and let control emerge. | Believe in yourself, your abilities, that you have continually refined as a teacher, that you are the one in control. It is your classroom, the students are in your charge. You are in control of your lesson. Know that you are the one in control, as a conductor controls an orchestra. |
| Loss of self-consciousness | If you are focusing on the task in hand, there will be no space left in your mind for self-consciousness ('How do I look?') or self-concern ('Am I doing this right?') or self-doubt ('Can I do this at all?'). When you gain a sense of control you will lose self-consciousness. This is a good thing! Avoid worrying about yourself, your lesson, what you should have done, or | Focus on the task in hand, the actual art of teaching. Avoid worrying. Just teach! |

*(Continued)*

**Table 13.1**    (Continued)

| Conditions of flow | Description | Example to facilitate each element |
|---|---|---|
| | should be doing. This will then free you up to engage fully in the actual process of teaching. You will be working on instinct. | |
| Merging of action and awareness | You mind and body become one. There is no separation between what you are thinking and what you are doing. Everything is just 'happening' naturally. | Try not to force anything to happen. Being focused on the present will enable you to feel this sense of 'merging'. |
| Transformation of time | Dependence on time is a burden. We continually refer to our watches, struggle to meet deadlines and cram the curriculum into the timetable, etc. This prevents us from engaging fully in our daily life. When you get into the classroom for the term, you should avoid mentally counting down the time. To achieve flow, time should not matter (although ensuring your pace may be useful for goal setting). If you mentally count down the time left, it will drag (think of waiting for a kettle to boil). If you are in flow, time seems to speed up (so you get to the end of the lesson before you realize it). | As noted above, keep focused on the present. Although the day works on a set timetable in school, you still have a lot of autonomy within your lesson as to how this is used. As long as the students are learning and you are teaching by keeping in the present, being in control, that students are engaged, then the time is yours! |

As an outcome of the flow experience, there is positive affect and self-affirmation. By this, flow is rewarding in its own right: as such, you want to experience this feeling time and time again.

 **Activity 13.3**

Review your description you noted for Activity 13.2.

Having read through the 'ingredients' of flow, revisit your description. Can you correlate any of the 'ingredients' to what happened (for example, the skill/challenge, etc.) Make a note of these.

An alternative, or perhaps complementary, way of exploring flow states is to use the Flow State Scale (FSS), which is a measure of flow in sport and physical activity settings developed by Susan Jackson and Mihalyi Csikszentmihalyi (1999). The questions in Activity 13.4 are derived from this scale and aim to give you a rough indication of whether you had entered 'the zone' in any of your lessons. Don't worry if some of the questions appear to be asking the same thing.

## Activity 13.4

Answer the questions below, which are derived from the FSS, after a specific lesson. Note the amount of times you have answered Yes and compare these against the amount of times you have answered No. Complete the scale for different lessons every few weeks to assess how your skills are developing and the value you have obtained from this book.

|  | Yes | No |
|---|---|---|
| Did my ability match the high challenge of the lesson? |  |  |
| Did I believe that my skills would allow me to meet the challenge? |  |  |
| Did I feel that I was competent enough to meet the high demands of the lesson? |  |  |
| *If you mainly answered 'Yes', you appear to have had the correct balance between challenge and skill.* |  |  |
| Did I teach on 'autopilot' thinking automatically? |  |  |
| Did I employ the correct teaching techniques without thinking about trying to do so? |  |  |
| Did I act spontaneously without having to think? |  |  |
| *If you mainly answered 'Yes', you appear to have been able to merge action with awareness.* |  |  |
| Did I know clearly what I wanted to do? |  |  |
| Were my goals clearly outlined? |  |  |
| Did I know exactly what I wanted to achieve during the lesson? |  |  |
| *If you mainly answered 'Yes', you appear to have had clear goals and were able to meet those goals.* |  |  |

*(Continued)*

*(Continued)*

|  | Yes | No |
|---|---|---|
| Was it clear that I was doing well during the lesson? | | |
| Did I know that I was achieving my objective? | | |
| Did I know how successfully I was teaching? | | |
| *If you mainly answered 'Yes', you appear to have been able to obtain feedback on your performance.* | | |
| Was I able to keep my mind on what was happening effortlessly? | | |
| Did I have total concentration? | | |
| Was I completely focused on the job of teaching? | | |
| *If you mainly answered 'No', you appear to have been able to concentrate and focus on your performance.* | | |
| Did I feel in total control of my teaching? | | |
| Did I feel that I could control exactly what I was doing? | | |
| Did I feel in complete control of my actions? | | |
| *If you mainly answered 'Yes', you appear to have been able to exercise control over your performance.* | | |
| Was I concerned with what others may have been thinking of me? | | |
| Was I worried about my performance during the lesson? | | |
| Was I concerned with how I was presenting myself during the lesson? | | |
| *If you mainly answered 'No', you appear to have been able to overcome the feeling of 'self-consciousness'.* | | |
| Did it feel as if time didn't seem to matter? | | |
| Did it feel as if time had stopped while I was teaching? | | |
| Did it seem as things were happening in slow motion at times during the lesson? | | |
| *If you mainly answered 'Yes', you appear to have been able to override the importance of time.* | | |
| Did the experience leave me feeling great? | | |
| Did I enjoy the feeling of that lesson and want to recapture it? | | |

|  | Yes | No |
|---|---|---|
| Did I find the experience extremely rewarding? |  |  |
| *You appear to have been able to experience the feeling of 'just doing it'!* |  |  |

The more questions you have answered 'Yes' to, the more likely it is that you were experiencing a 'flow state'. If you have answered 'No' to most of the questions, don't worry. At least you have more of an idea of the kind of elements that may help you to get into a 'flow state' during lessons in the future.

## Final comment

If you begin to think in this way, the rewards will just come as a consequence of your achieving flow states. Nothing else matters, only doing this for the 'right' reasons.

There is a notion that teachers should strive for perfection or that they are perfectionists. Perfection does not exist except in one's mind! Flow provides a glimpse of it. Flow is perhaps the closest to perfection that a teacher is likely to attain. Imagine that teaching 'perfection' is represented by a narrow line or path, which you 'fall off' if you don't get it right. Flow is more like operating within a 'window of opportunity'. There are many ways through a situation, *not* a right or wrong way. Flow will allow you to perform within this window while other teachers are becoming self-conscious because they are not balancing their work effectively.

We would advise teachers to avoid getting bogged down with the terminology outlined in the nine steps above. Rather, you should try to build the practical information into preparations for teaching. If you *try* too hard, you will not achieve flow!

The final statement we have to make is that although you have reached the end of this book, you will undoubtedly have reached the beginning of your journey of discovery. The performance profile from the previous chapter along with the various explorative questions dotted around the chapters will act as a foundation for future progress. The guidance provided in each of the preceding chapters should feed into the database of performance profiles, journal entries, goal-setting sheets and any other sheets of paper that you have accumulated at this point, to help you move forward in your chosen career.

Remain focused, remain positive and build on your existing skills, whether you are reading this as a novice or a highly experienced teacher … and remember that an improvement the size of a grain of salt is still an improvement and a move in the right direction.

## One-minute summary

Perspective has been an implicit theme throughout this book. As such, if you can see yourself as 'stuck', is this a rut or a plateau? We have also looked at the concept of 'flow', a state that we can probably all identify with at some time or another, yet often by accident. Csikszentmihalyi provides information on the elements that facilitate 'flow', which with a little thought, can be applied to your teaching. This in turn leads to intrinsic motivation for your career and for continuing to strive to be the best teacher possible.

Remember that this book is to be **worked with** and not just read. Only through engaging with the various activities can you bring this book to life. Welcome to your homework! Engaging, enjoyable and educationally stimulating!

## Short-term strategies for the here and now

- Review Activity 13.1 to regain a perspective on the plateau.
- Consider a time when you have been in the 'flow' state … when everything went 'right' and you were lost in the moment. This may not necessarily be in your teaching. However, reflecting on the feeling, while also reviewing the elements of flow can help you experience this with your teaching.
- Identify areas on Activity 13.4 that you could work with. Ensure you set realistic goals.

## Mentoring issues

Discuss with your mentor if you feel you have reached a plateau and do not know what direction would be best. Consider the various options that are open, and discuss each of these in turn with your mentor. By vocalizing these, the next step may become evident.

Discuss with your mentor the 'flow' state, specifically if you feel the skill–challenge balance is weighted in excess one way or the other. Discuss what could be altered in order to enable your skills to meet the challenge or the challenge to meet your skills.

# 📖 Further reading

The 'father of flow' is Mihalyi Csikszentmihalyi. He has written numerous books on the subject, all of which provide variation on the theme. One book which effectively summarizes his (and others) work on flow is:

Csikszentmihalyi, M. (2008) *Flow: The Psychology of Optimal Experience*. London: Harper Perennial.
This book provides general principles and examples of flow and is not a step-by-step guide on achieving flow. There is however a more 'practical' guide available:

Csikszentmihalyi, M. (1998) *Finding Flow: The Psychology of Engagement with Everyday Life*. Jackson, TN: Basic Books.

# References

Bandura, A. (1977) *Social-learning Theory*. New York: Prentice-Hall.

Beadle, P. (2008) *Could Do Better: Help Your Kid Shine At School*. London: Corgi Books.

Blackwell, R. (2003) *Guidelines for Promoting and Facilitating Change*. York: Learning and Teaching Support Network Generic Centre.

Butler, R.J. and Hardy, L. (1992) 'The performance profile: theory and application', *The Sport Psychologist*, 6: 253–64.

Castle, P.C., Van Toller, S. and Milligan, G.J. (2000) 'The Effects of odour priming on cortical EEG and visual ERP responses', *International Journal of Psychophysiology*, 36: 121–31.

Craine, K. (2007) 'Managing the cycle of change', *The Information Management Journal*, September/October: 44–50.

Csikszentmihalyi, M. (2000) 'The contribution of flow to positive psychology: scientific essays in honour of Martin E.P. Seligman', in J.E. Gillham (ed.), *The Science of Optimism and Hope*. Philadelphia, PA: Templeton Foundation Press.

Csikszentmihalyi, M. (2008) *Flow: The Psychology of Optimal Experience*. London: Harper Perennial.

Daniels, M. (2005) *Shadow, Self, Spirit: Essays in Transpersonal Psychology*. Exeter: Imprint Academic.

Deci, E.L. and Ryan, R.M. (1985) *Intrinsic Motivation and Self-Determination in Human Behaviour*. New York: Plenum.

Department for Education and Employment (DfEE) (2000) *Fitness to Teach: Occupational Health Guidance for the Training and Employment of Teachers*. Norwich: HMSO.

Easterbrook, J.A. (1959) 'The effect of emotion on cue utilisation and the organisation of behaviour', *Psychological Review*, 66: 183–201.

Ellis, A. (1962) *Reason and Emotion in Psychotherapy*. New York: Lyle Stuart.

Fazey, J. and Hardy, L. (1988) 'The inverted-U hypothesis: catastrophe for sport psychology', *British Association for Sports Sciences Monograph*, No.1. Leeds: The National Coaching Foundation.

Godden, D. and Baddeley, A.D. (1975) 'Context-dependent memory in two natural environments: on land and under water', *British Journal of Psychology*, 66: 325–31.

Handy, C. (1993) *Understanding Organisations*. 4th edn. London: Penguin.

Hritz, C. (2008) 'Change model: three stages to success', *Leadership Excellence*, May: 14.

Hull, C.L. (1943) *Principles of Behaviour*. New York: Appleton-Century-Crofts Inc.

Jackson, S.A. and Csikszentmihalyi, M. (1999) *Flow in Sports: The Keys to Optimal Experiences and Performances*. Champaign, IL: Human Kinetics.

Jacobson, E. (1938) *Progressive Relaxation*. 2nd edn. Chicago, IL: University of Chicago Press.

James, W. (1890) *Principles of Psychology*. Vol. 1. New York: Henry Holt.

Jones, G. (1995) 'More than just a game: research developments and issues in competitive anxiety in sport', *British Journal of Psychology*, 86: 449–478.

Klicka, J., Kolumbus, R. and Weber, B. (2006) 'Video games for the improvement of reaction time and hand eye coordination in college football players', *Journal of Undergraduate Kinesiology*, 2(1): 55–63.

Krüger, W. (2002) *Excellence in Change*. Wiesbaden: Gabler.

Kubler-Ross, E. and Kessler, D. (2005) *On Grief and Grieving: Finding the Meaning of Grief Through the Five Stages of Loss*. London: Simon and Schuster.

Lavallee, D., Kremer, J., Moran, A.P. and Williams, M. (2004) *Sport Psychology: Contemporary Themes*. New York: Palgrave Macmillan.

Loehr, J.E. (1995) *The New Mental Toughness Training for Sports*. New York: Penguin.

Martens, R., Burton, D., Vealey, R.S., Bump, L.A. and Smith, D. (1990) 'Development and validation of the Competitive State Anxiety Inventory-2', in R. Martens, R.S. Vealey and D. Burton (eds), *Competitive Anxiety in Sport*. Champaign, IL: Human Kinetics.

Maslow, A.H. (1970) *Motivation and Personality*. 2nd edn. New York: Harper and Row.

McCarthy, P.J. (2009) 'Putting imagery to good affect: a case study among youth swimmers', *Sport and Exercise Psychology Review*, 5(1): 27–38.

Moran, A.P. (1996) *The Psychology of Concentration in Sport Performers: A Cognitive Analysis*. Hove: Psychology Press.

NASUWT (2008) *Safe to Teach? Final Report of the NASUWT Survey on Health and Safety in Schools and Colleges*. Birmingham: Clarkprint.

Nideffer, R.M. (1976) 'Test of attentional and interpersonal style', *Journal of Personality and Social Psychology*, 34: 394–404.

Paivio, A. (1985) 'Cognitive and motivational functions of imagery in human performance', *Canadian Journal of Applied Sport Sciences*, 10: 225–85.

Pennington, G. (2003) *Guidelines for Promoting and Facilitating Change*. York: Learning and Teaching Support Network (LTSN).

Prochaska, J.O. and DiClemente, C.C. (1983) 'Stages and processes of self-change of smoking: toward an integrative model of change', *Journal of Consulting and Clinical Psychology*, 51: 390–5.

Schön, D. (1983) *The Reflective Practitioner*. New York: Basic Books.

Schultz, J.H. and Luthe, W. (1959) *Autogenic Training: A Psychophysiological Approach to Psychotherapy*. New York: Grune and Stratton.

Seligman, M.E.P. (1975) *Helplessness: On Depression, Development, and Death*. San Francisco, CA: W.H. Freeman.

Selye, H. (1956) *The Stress of Life*. New York: McGraw-Hill.

Selye, H. (1983) 'The stress concept: past, present and future', in C.L. Cooper (ed.), *Stress Research*. New York: Wiley.

Smith, M.J. (1975) *When I Say No, I Feel Guilty: How to Cope Using the Skills of Systematic Assertive Therapy*. London: Bantam.

Taylor, R.J. and Berry, E. (1998) 'The use of a computer game to rehabilitate sensorimo-tor functional deficits following a subarachnoid haemorrhage', *Neuropsychology Rehabilitation*, 8(2): 113–22.

Thorndike, E.L. (1920) 'A constant error on psychological rating', *Journal of Applied Psychology*, 4: 25–9.

Vallerand, R.J. (2001) 'A Hierarchical Model of Intrinsic and Extrinsic Motivation in Sport and Exercise', in, G.C. Roberts (ed.), *Advances in Motivation in Sport and Exercise*. Champaign: Human Kinetics.

Van Toller, S. (2009) *The Nose and I*. (Forthcoming.)

Vealey, R.S. (1986) 'Conceptualisation of sport-confidence and competitive orienta-tion: preliminary investigation and instrument development', *Journal of Sport Psychology*, 8: 221–246.

Weinberg, R.S. and Gould, D. (2007) *Foundations of Sport and Exercise Psychology*. 4th edn. Champaign, IL: Human Kinetics.

West, J. (2005) '"Energising" mental imagery script', University of Worcester Student handout (unpublished).

Williams, J.M. and Harris, D.V. (2006) 'Relaxation and energizing techniques for regulation of arousal', in J.M. Williams (ed.), *Applied Sport Psychology: Personal Growth to Peak Performance*. 5th edn. Mountain View, CA: Mayfield.

Yerkes, R.M. and Dodson, J.D. (1908) 'The relation of strength of stimulus to rapidity of habit-formation', *Journal of Comparative Neurology and Psychology*, 18: 459–82.

# Index